MAN'S MARVELOUS COMPUTER:

The Next Quarter Century

Richard B. Rusch

SIMON AND SCHUSTER, NEW YORK

TO TODD SHAPTER RUSCH

Contents

Acknowledgments

Through the centuries man has often been fearful of what his inventions would do to him. When the first wheel was crudely fashioned someone probably thought he had lost a job, and after the wheel was attached to a cart and an ox was used to pull it, someone else was worried about his future.

This fear reached a high point during the Industrial Revolution, but it later diminished when it became apparent that technology was creating more jobs than it was destroying. In the 1950's, the fear again appeared, this time with the introduction of computers.

But computers are not like other machines, limited to a single task in a factory or office. Rapidly, they are becoming a way of life, influencing not only employment but the direction of society itself.

This book briefly explains the history and operation of computers, then predicts some of their more important future uses. By recognizing these uses now, it is hoped that the people of this nation, and the world, will act to solve the social and psychological problems which could be created.

These predictions are based on statements made by educators, government officials, scientists, research engineers, sociologists and psychologists, and also on personal study of hundreds of computer installations. Illustrative material in the first two chapters has been taken in part from my previous book on computers; illustrations for the rest of the book have been obtained through the assistance of International Business Machines Corporation and the Computer Systems Division of RCA Corporation.

To the people who have helped me, and to IBM and RCA, I am deeply grateful.

RICHARD B. RUSCH

MAN'S MARVELOUS COMPUTER:

The Next Quarter Century

I

One Computer,
Many Fingers

The date is Election Day, somewhere between 1976 and the year 2000.

During previous elections you listened to the TV speeches, read your newspaper, then braved the crowds at the voting booths to cast your ballot. But not today. Speeches, though important, are no longer the major source of information about a candidate; newspapers have pretty much disappeared, and ballots are cast right in your own home, using touch-tone telephones connected to an election-center computer.

This computer, which will record your ballot, has also provided much of the information enabling you to choose a candidate. Using the touch-tone telephone, you first instructed the computer to display on a television screen connected to your telephone a profile of the personal, educational and vocational backgrounds of each of the candidates, their past legislative experience, and their current policy positions. In those cases where you have not been able to make a selection based on this information, you have gone back to the computer with more detailed questions. How has each man previously voted on foreign aid? Civil rights? Crime control? Taxation? Urban development? Armaments? Pollution? What bills has he introduced in Congress? In the state legislature? In the county or locally? What was the text of these bills? How many were passed? How many were defeated? How many were vetoed? Almost any question you could ask about a particular candidate, the computer was able to answer.

This election procedure is not as impossible as it sounds, for you are in the computer world of the next quarter century, a world where man and machine come together. In this world of tomorrow you will see many computers serving many people: answering their questions; helping to solve their mathematical, scientific, social, economic or business problems; providing the information they need to make correct, frequently instantaneous, decisions.

In this coming era, the computer may make it possible for students sitting at keyboards to answer questions provided by a computer rather than a teacher; for housewives to purchase groceries, clothing and other merchandise, yet seldom enter a store; for doctors to diagnose illnesses without ever seeing the patient; for engineers to design buildings, but rarely draft a blueprint; and for people to pay bills, yet never exchange money.

You may also witness mammoth cities entirely free of traffic congestion, interplanetary spacecraft guided solely by voice command, 150-mile-per-hour commuter trains operated without human direction, 200-story skyscrapers constructed by a labor force of less than 80 workers, and laws enforced by a nationwide network of "electronic" policemen.

Toward the end of the 20th century, homes and cars may have their own computers. One English scientist even predicts that by the year 2000 every person may wear a computer no larger than a wrist watch run by the body's electrical energy and capable of recording a lifetime volume of useful information.

All these advances, and others, are not only possible but probable, for much of the technology needed to accomplish them is already available or soon will be. How these advances might affect your future is, however, less easy to predict, since most of the nation's people have never used a computer.

Because of this lack of experience, many individuals fear the computer. They think of it as a cold, impersonal machine which reduces human identities to nothing more than a set of numbers. Some dislike the computer because it sometimes makes unreasonable mistakes; others, because it may cost them their jobs; and still others, because they are afraid it will bring about a society in which privacy is nonexistent and freedom of choice is the prerogative of the computer's directors.

Such fears are based on the fact that computers, by the very way they operate, *do* designate people as numbers; that they are capable of recording vast quantities of personal information; that they do, at times, repeat a mistake; that they can replace man in many jobs; and that they are usually housed in isolated chambers where, to the general public, they seem distant and unapproachable.

People usually lose these fears, however, once they understand the purpose of computers, and know how computers can make their lives easier and their jobs more enjoyable. Ever since man appeared on this planet, he has sought to improve his life by accumulating and applying knowledge. In primitive times, this knowledge was gained through observation of natural phenomena followed by a period of trial and error. The caveman who was freezing, for example, discovered that the embers of a tree set on fire by lightning could ignite a stack of wood in his dwelling, and that this fire would keep him warm. By building fires of different types of woods, he eventually found out which type of wood burned the hottest and the longest, which type of wood was good for kindling, and which type of wood would not burn at all.

Little by little, man expanded his knowledge of the world

around him. New knowledge led to new discoveries, and new discoveries led to still more knowledge. Today, this build-up of knowledge has reached a point where man, in the past thirty years, has accumulated more knowledge about the world and the universe in which he lives than he had accumulated in all the preceding centuries. And by 1985 it is expected that he will know twice as much as he knows today!

This knowledge-explosion presents a problem, for knowledge today is often such that man cannot decide the proper way to apply the information he has compiled. This usually happens in one of four cases: When the amount of information is more than man can comprehend; when the information itself is changing even while man is attempting to understand it; when a decision must be made faster than man's ability to analyze the information; or when all the preceding conditions exist simultaneously.

An illustration of the first situation is typically encountered by students striving to learn all the information presented in all the textbooks used in all the courses taken during each school year. Although the attempt is made, few if any students actually succeed, for the amount of information is just too much for a student's brain to understand and remember.

Two people playing a game of chess in which a special rule requires each move to be made within thirty seconds present an illustration of the second situation. In this speeded-up version of the game, played by some people as a means of mental stimulation, the information itself is changing even while the players are attempting to understand it. Both opponents surely will find it difficult to make correct decisions, since it is impossible for them to determine all the consequences of an opponent's move in such a limited amount of time. In the standard game of chess, where hours are sometimes spent analyzing positions and projecting the consequences of just one move, reaching a correct decision is much more likely.

The third situation is exemplified by numerous traffic accidents on our nation's highways every day. If the brain had time to study the predicament the driver faces, and if his reflexes could react quickly enough, many accidents could possibly be avoided. Rather than stepping on the brake, one might do better, for instance, to speed up, or to cut the wheel hard to the right or to the left. But since the car is traveling so fast, the human brain cannot determine the proper action to take, and the collision occurs.

Finally, there is the situation where all the preceding conditions exist simultaneously. Controlling the flight of a spacecraft moving between 17,000 and 25,000 miles per hour is one example of this. The volume of operating information is obviously more than man can fathom; ascent and orbit positions are changing faster than man can track them; and flight-correction decisions must be made faster than man can make them.

These, then, are the reasons why man uses the computer. He needs it to aid in the accumulation and analysis of information, regardless of its volume or condition, and to provide the facts needed to make correct decisions in a specific time-span. By turning these jobs over to the computer, man can also free himself of the drudgery of gathering and sorting information, which is what most jobs today involve, and can gain more time in which to apply his creative abilities. While it may appear that he has put himself out of a job, he actually has created two or more new positions to replace the old one, and these are positions offering him opportunity for greater responsibility and self-fulfillment if he is qualified to fill them.

In some of these new jobs, man can have the computer make decisions for him. But this does not mean a computer can think. The computer can only accumulate and store information provided by man, or in some cases by another machine; sort and analyze that information according to instructions given by man; and furnish the result or results in a manner best enabling man to decide what action to take. Only when man instructs the computer to do something when certain conditions are met, will he allow the computer to initiate an action directly. These conditions will be a series of questions posed by man which the computer will answer with a "yes" or a "no." For example, to approve a person's credit purchase, the computer might answer the question "Will this customer be within his authorized credit limit with this purchase?" Adding the cost of the purchase to credit amounts previously recorded and still unpaid, the computer will determine "Yes, the customer is within his credit limit with this purchase," or "No, he exceeds it." When the answer is "yes," the computer will approve the purchase; when the answer is "no," it will reject it.

With today's computers almost any type of information can be handled. It can be business, agricultural, weather, banking, or educational information, social service, medical, battlefield or crime information. Today's computers also can recognize nearly every form of information: mathematical or alphabetical, spoken or drawn.

Sometimes a computer will make an error in the performance of its duties. But such errors usually are no more the fault of the computer than writing a wrong answer on an exam is the fault of the pencil; it is just that the original information entered into the computer (or into your brain) was wrong to begin with. And unless this wrong information is corrected, the computer always will come up with a wrong answer.

It is the difficulty of correcting wrong information once it is in the computer that causes many people to turn against the use of computers. It sometimes happens that a person finds a mistake on a bill; he contacts a company service representative to correct the error, only to find that the next month's bill contains the same mistake or some other mistake. What has happened is that the service representative has had to tell someone working with the computer to correct the records, and this person either has not yet made the correction or has made the correction in the wrong way.

In the future there will undoubtedly be fewer and fewer of these "man-made" computer errors. And in those instances when an error does occur, man will be able to isolate its exact location and cause more easily and quickly. This will be accomplished in part through improvements in the computer's own error-checking capability. But to a greater extent it will be accomplished by using computer communications devices resembling television sets and typewriters. These will make possible direct access to and use of the computer by people familiar with the information, rather than only by computer-room personnel.

Currently, information usually is prepared for computer entry by these computer-room workers. They take information from a source document, such as a customer order, a check, or a credit application form, and enter it to a machine which translates the information into a language which the computer can understand. Since these people do not always understand the information they are handling, there is room for error.

Eventually, as computers improve and become easier to use, everyone, from architect to zoologist, from preschooler to grandparent, will be able to enter information to a computer himself, rather than having to work through a second party. Thus the margin for error will be greatly reduced. Also, if there is an error, it will be possible for the person familiar with the information to isolate the spot where the error is located and to make the necessary corrections. Before this can happen, however, there will have to be communications instruments, tied to the computer, located in virtually every home, office, school and store, and even perhaps on street corners . . . in effect, one computer with many fingers.

How, though, can a person become a competent user of computer power if he has never before used a computer and has no idea of how it works?

The answer, of course, is education: learning what a

computer is, how it operates, and how it can be made to perform the many actions which man desires it to perform. If man can learn this, and he certainly will be given the opportunity, then, we may hope, he can also learn how the computer can best be used to benefit himself as well as the society in which he lives.

II
Background on
the Future

Few people are aware that man's first step in the development of mechanized information processing took place some 3,000 to 3,500 years ago. This occurred with the invention of the abacus—not by the Chinese, as most people believe, but perhaps rather by the Greeks or Egyptians, since the word *abacus* seems to be a derivative of the Greek word *abax,* meaning "board" or "slab."

Probably the Greek or Egyptian version of the abacus was indeed a board or slab covered with sand or dust, with marks fingered in this material indicating a particular quantity. The Chinese version of the abacus, however, is a box separated into an upper and a lower compartment. Beads strung on rods in the upper compartment each represent a value of five, and beads strung on rods in the lower compartment each represent a value of one. The value of a number is shown by moving the beads toward a board separating the two compartments.

While some people still use the abacus today for business and mathematical calculations, it fell from general favor as a computational device around 1400 A.D.—mainly as a

On the Chinese abacus, beads that move on rods are separated by a counting board into two compartments. Each bead in the top compartment has a value of five, and each bead in the lower compartment has a value of one. Counting is accomplished by moving beads toward the counting board.

result of the appearance of paper and the widespread acceptance of the Arabic-numeral system of counting, still used today in almost every part of the world.

By the early 1600's, Western man became dissatisfied with the slow, tedious and error-prone procedures of writing numbers on paper. So, around 1640, a French mathematician, Blaise Pascal, developed an adding machine which operated in a manner similar to today's automobile odometer, the dashboard instrument which indicates the number of miles traveled. In Pascal's adding machine, a series of small toothed wheels, set side by side, were marked from 0 to 9 on the perimeter. When a wheel completed a revolution from 0 to 9 and came back to 0 again, it automatically moved the wheel on its left forward one digit.

Since Pascal's machine could only add, it could not be used for all computational problems. About 1690, however, a man named Gottfried von Leibniz developed a calculator which could both multiply and divide as well as add.

Today, almost every business office uses some improved version of Pascal's adding machine and Leibniz's calculator. But these instruments are not effective for the solution of *all* mathematical problems: first, because they require that a key be punched every time a number is to be added, subtracted, multiplied or divided—and for complex equations this can be exceedingly time consuming; and second, because they require that answers to one problem be copied down or remembered if they are to be applied in some other problem.

A step in eliminating each of these drawbacks was taken in 1801 when Joseph Jacquard developed an automatic weaving loom. Jacquard punched into cards or paper tape the operating instructions needed to control the patterns woven by the loom. Though not a calculating device, his brainchild was the beginning step in representing pieces of information by the arrangement of holes in cards or in long pieces of paper. This procedure, utilizing the now familiar punched card, is still employed for entering information to most computers. These pieces of information are now referred to as *data* (the plural of *datum,* literally "something given").

The next major advance in the development of the computer was made by a young Englishman named Charles Babbage. In 1823, he persuaded the British government to finance the building of an invention he called the "Difference Engine." This machine was designed to compute lengthy but not necessarily complex mathematical problems and to print the results in the form of tables.

Using the principles of his "Difference Engine," Babbage next developed a device called an "Analytical Engine" that could do what modern computers do—that is, accept a problem, produce answers according to given instructions, store the results, and print out final answers. But Babbage was born 130 years too soon. The technology of his day was not advanced enough to mass-produce the parts his

The "Difference Engine," built by Charles Babbage in 1823, was man's first digital computer. Though not completely reliable, this machine was able to receive a problem, calculate answers based on given instructions, store results and print out answers.

machine needed, and when Babbage died he had only one small working model of the "Analytical Engine" to his credit.

Before he died, however, Babbage met Lady Lovelace,

the daughter of Lord Byron. Recognizing the potential of Babbage's work, this young woman, a genius in mathematics, devised a form of "binary arithmetic" using just two digits, the 1 and the 0, which is still used in computers today. But even her work, ingenious as it was, did not help promote the promise of Babbage's machine.

Not until some fifty years later did the course of computer development take the next significant step forward. This occurred when nineteen-year-old Herman Hollerith, an employee of the Census Bureau of the United States Department of the Interior, developed what he called a "Census Machine," a completely mechanical device which

By using Herman Hollerith's Census Machine, built in 1890, the time required for processing census data was reduced by almost two-thirds. It was not a computer, since it simply totaled identical data—such as the number of people who were doctors—but it used many of the operating principles found in modern data-processing systems.

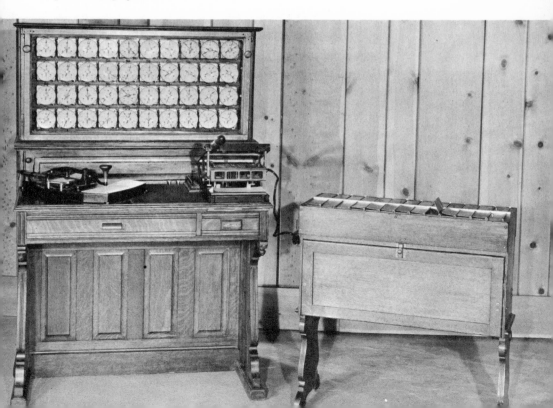

used punched cards for data tabulation. Then Hollerith created an electrical and mechanical (electro-mechanical) machine he called an Electric Tabulating System. This machine was first used to compile population statistics for the Census of 1890; it reduced the time required to process the census information by almost five years.

During the latter part of the nineteenth century and the first thirty years of the twentieth century, the United States moved rapidly forward into the technological era. Railroads were opened throughout the nation, mass production became the byword in factory after factory, and tons of manufactured materials flowed from one mechanized shop to another. Electro-mechanical data-processing machines which were fed data by punched cards kept pace with these advances and helped to control the exploding volumes of information.

But electro-mechanical punched-card machines ultimately proved too slow and inflexible to handle the growing processing requirements, particularly in jobs which required extensive mathematical computation. To meet these needs, a Harvard professor named Howard Aiken conceived and developed the first of man's modern computers. In 1937, he took a complex of 78 adding machines and desk calculators, all controlled by instructions punched into paper tape, and created a data-processing device known as the Automatic Sequence Controlled Calculator, or Harvard Mark I. Completed in 1944, the machine could multiply and divide as well as tabulate. Once processing began, no further human involvement was required.

Even Aiken's creation, which could perform about three additions or three subtractions in one second, was not fast enough. In 1946, Dr. J. Presper Eckert, Jr., and Dr. John W. Mauchly of the University of Pennsylvania developed an all-electronic vacuum-tube computer. Since this computer involved no mechanical movement of parts as did the Harvard Mark I, it speeded the processing of data tremen-

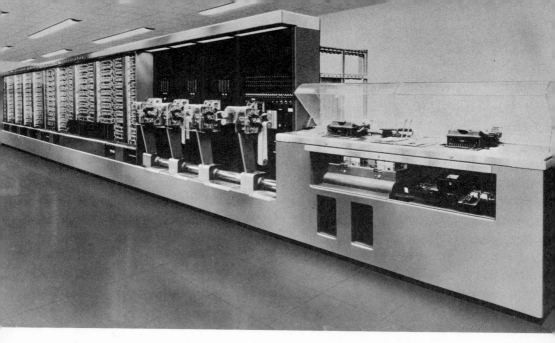

Howard Aiken's Harvard Mark I is considered the first digital computer capable of completely automatic operation. It consists of a complex of 78 adding machines and desk calculators controlled by instructions punched onto a roll of paper tape.

dously. Known as ENIAC (Electronic Numerical Integrator and Calculator), the Eckert-Mauchly machine could perform 5,000 additions in one second!

Since then, computers have become even faster, more flexible, and more easily controlled. A computer today is not just one instrument, but rather a group of interacting instruments which, taken all together, are known as a "computer system."

Five main activities are carried out by the computer system: input, storage, control, processing and output. *Input* means entering data to the computer or central processor, as it is sometimes called. *Storage* is holding the data for future use either in the computer itself or in "memory" devices attached to the computer. *Control* is "telling" the computer precisely what to do and how and in what order by feeding a set of instructions, called a program, into the memory unit of the computer. *Processing* is the actual manipulation of data within the computer. *Output* is the presentation of final results.

In today's computers, use of small electronic (microelectronic) circuits in place of vacuum tubes has resulted in operating speeds that stagger the imagination. In the early and middle 1950's a data-processing execution in a thousandth of a second (one millisecond) was news. Today, computers perform the same execution in a billionth of a second (a *nanosecond. Nano* means *dwarf* or *midget*). And five or ten years from now they may do it in a trillionth of a second.

The cost of computers in terms of efficiency also has improved immensely. In 1950, one dollar bought 35,000 data-processing executions. Today, a dollar buys over 35 million. It has been said, in fact, that in the past ten years computers have become ten times smaller, one hundred times faster, and one thousand times less expensive.

Interestingly, though, representation of data fed to the computer often is based on the very concept of binary arithmetic devised by Lady Lovelace more than a century ago. Indeed, the binary number system is precisely the means which enables the computer to manipulate and store virtually any type of information.

The electronic components of the different devices making up the computer system can indicate one of only two possible conditions at any time. This is known as the "binary mode," meaning that there are two and only two conditions involved (from *bi,* meaning two). The binary mode can be illustrated by an ordinary light bulb which is either "on" (producing light) or "off" (not producing light). Because the binary arithmetic system operates in the same mode in that it uses only two digits, zero and one, to express all numbers, it is used in most computers, rather than some other system, such as the decimal system, which uses ten digits to express all numbers.

Using the system of binary arithmetic developed by Lady

Today's computer systems are 10 times smaller, 100 times faster, and 1,000 times less expensive than computer systems built in 1960. Tomorrow's computer systems will be even smaller, faster and less expensive than current equipment.

Lovelace, man can translate numbers and alphabetic and special characters (for example, $, #, %, etc.) into the binary mode so that the computer system can process the information.

As we've already seen, in the binary arithmetic system, all numbers are expressed using only two digits, 0 and 1. This differs from the more commonly used decimal system (from *deci,* meaning ten) in which the ten digits from 0 through 9 are used to express all numbers. The first and second binary digits, as in the decimal system, are 0 and 1. But there the similarity stops. In the binary system, the decimal number 2 is represented by the next larger binary number, 10. The next binary number after 10 is 11, and this represents the next larger decimal number, 3. Here is a chart showing how the first ten numbers of the decimal system are written in binary form:

Decimal	Binary
0	0
1	1
2	10
3	11
4	100
5	101
6	110
7	111
8	1000
9	1001

The decimal equivalent of a binary number can be obtained by multiplying each digit in the binary number by its place value. In the decimal system, the place value of each digit, reading from right to left, is a multiple of ten:

Ten Thousands   Thousands   Hundreds   Tens   Ones

In the binary system, the place value of each digit moving from right to left is a multiple of two:

Sixteens   Eights   Fours   Twos   Ones

To obtain the decimal equivalent of the binary number 1101, then, each of the digits is multiplied by its place value as follows:

Eights	*Fours*	*Twos*	*Ones*
1	1	0	1

$$(1 \times 8) \ + \ (1 \times 4) \ + \ (0 \times 2) \ + \ (1 \times 1)$$

$$8 \ + \ 4 \ + \ 0 \ + \ 1 = 13$$

Binary numbers can be added, subtracted, multiplied and divided, just like decimal numbers. For example, the decimal numbers 4 plus 4 (100 plus 100 in binary form) can be added in binary form as shown below:

$$
\begin{array}{r}
100 \\
+\,100 \\
\hline
200
\end{array}
$$

Since there is no digit 2 in the binary system, a zero is put in its place and a 1 is carried to the next column to the left, making the final answer 1000 or the equivalent of the decimal number 8.

The binary system is also used in computers to represent letters of the alphabet and special characters as well as numbers. The letters and special characters are first coded and then translated to their binary equivalents. The word "buy," for instance, might be coded as the decimal number 345; it is then translated to the binary number 101011001, or possibly to a series of binary numbers depending on the design of the computer: 11 (the equivalent of the decimal number 3); 100 (the equivalent of the decimal number 4); and 101 (the equivalent of the decimal number 5).

Remember it was said earlier that the electronic components of the different devices of the computer system can indicate one of only two possible conditions at any one moment; that is, that they operate in a binary mode. When one of these components is turned "on," it represents the binary digit 1, and when it is turned "off," it represents the binary digit 0. When these components are grouped into sets, with some of the components in the set "on" and some of them "off," it is possible to represent an entire binary number.

In the computer, the components used to indicate these binary numbers are extremely minute ($2\frac{1}{1000}$ of an inch in diameter, or smaller), doughnut-shaped pieces of iron oxide material called magnetic cores. There can be thousands, hundreds of thousands or even millions of these cores in a single computer. They are strung on wires in such a way that each core is connected with every other core in the unit, but each still can be magnetized, demagnetized or "read" by an electrical current without affecting any other core. When one of these cores is magnetized, it can represent the binary digit "1"; and when not magnetized, the binary digit "0". Selective grouping of these cores by proper programming enables the computer to represent an entire binary

Magnetic cores, which are tiny rings of magnetic material about $\frac{21}{1000}$-inch in diameter, are used in most of today's high-speed computers. A computer can contain as few as eight thousand or as many as a million or more cores, depending on the size of the computer.

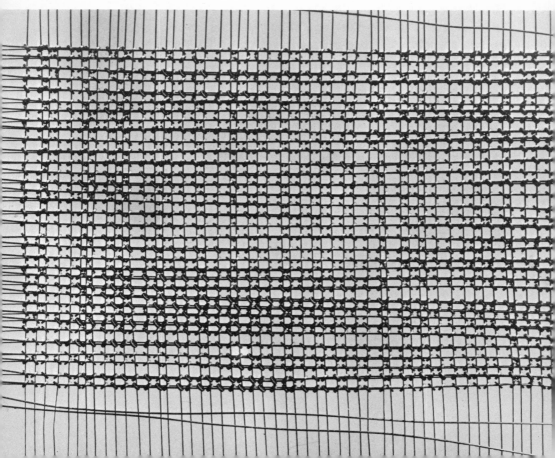

number, which can be compared, added and subtracted, just as a handwritten decimal number can be. (Since multiplication is no more than repeated addition, and division no more than repeated subtraction, the computer can also multiply and divide.)

Representing binary numbers on punched cards and punched paper tape, or on magnetic tape, magnetic disks and thin photographic films used in "memory" devices attached to the computer, is accomplished in much the same manner. With punched cards and punched paper tape the binary digit "1" is indicated by the presence of a hole, and with magnetic tape, magnetic disks and thin films by the presence of a magnetized spot. Conversely, the binary digit "0" is indicated by the absence of these holes or magnetized spots.

In some of today's advanced computer systems, the translation of decimal numbers and alphabetic and special characters to binary numbers can be handled by the computer itself. The need for first transcribing source information into binary form on punched cards, punched paper tape or magnetic tape is thus eliminated. The computers capable of performing this direct translation chore are those that have special communications devices—or terminals, as they are called—attached to them.

These terminals may take the form of typewriter units and television screens. On a typewriter terminal, each number, letter or special character typed on the keyboard generates a specific electrical pulse. On a television screen, a specific arrangement of dots is generated by a typewriter attached to the television set. The typewriter pulses and the location of television dots are read by electronic components in the computer and recorded in binary form to indicate the letter, number or special character that they represent. Using a special light pen, pictures also can be drawn on a television terminal, then stored in the computer by translating line locations on the TV screen to the binary mode. Output of

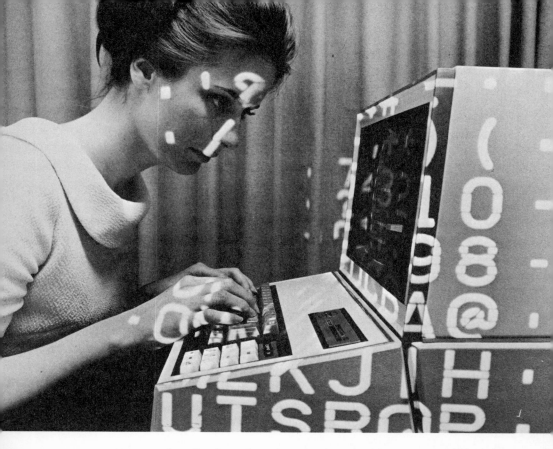

A typewriter keyboard with attached television screen makes it possible for data transmitted to or received from a remote computer to be visually displayed on the face of the terminal.

computer-processed or stored number, letter or special-character information to typewriter terminals and number, letter, special-character or drawing information to television terminals is accomplished by reversing the input procedure.

Increasing use of these terminals, coupled with vastly improved computer-processing speeds, information handling and storage capabilities, will play a predominant role in the upcoming evolution of computer usage. Indeed, the availability of such terminals is even now causing a major revision in the way computers are used and, consequently, a change of direction within the computer industry itself.

III

A Whole New Type
of Computer

From the time computers first appeared, the normal way of processing data was to transcribe source information into binary form on punched cards, group together those punched cards to be processed by the same computer program (a customer billing program, for example), and then feed the groups of cards one after another into the computer. This procedure, called batch processing, provides greater utilization of the computer by continuous manipulation of the same or similar information. What occurs is much like painting four different fences in identical colors. Obviously, it is more efficient to paint one fence after another using the same paint and paint brush than to paint one fence, close the paint can, clean the brush and tackle some other chore before starting to paint the second fence, the third fence, and then the fourth.

But batch processing, while it increases the efficiency of the computer, often presents the user with substantial problems in the long "turnaround" times it creates. Turnaround time is the total time required to deliver source information to the center where the computer is housed, have it transcribed to punched cards and processed by the computer, and then have the final results returned to the person needing the information.

To try to solve the problem of too-long turnaround time, the Massachusetts Institute of Technology in 1960 began work that led to a concept of computer utilization now known as time sharing. Using time sharing, a person no longer has to travel to the computer to process information or to wait for a specially trained person to operate the computer for him. Many people in different locations can employ a single computer simultaneously for a variety of processing needs.

In time sharing, the user communicates with the computer, using the terminal device best suited to his processing requirements. For example, a design engineer might use a special TV terminal enabling him to draw a bridge, a building or some other construction design on the face of the TV screen. He would make the drawing using an electronic pen, and the drawing itself would be transmitted to the computer. The computer might change the perspective of the drawing and relay this new view of the design back to the TV terminal for the engineer's use. An office manager might use a television terminal with a typewriter keyboard attached to it to input financial data about his company's business. The processed information would then be displayed on the terminal's screen as printed data useful for evaluation and application by the manager. A clerk in a retail store might use a terminal capable of reading credit card information. This information would be transferred to the computer, which could immediately validate the customer's credit standing and record the purchase information. A doctor might use a typewriter to input information about the symptoms of a patient's illness. The computer then could diagnose the illness and print its findings back on the doctor's terminal.

If a suitable program has been developed for the computer, it can handle almost any information received through almost any type of terminal. Furthermore, because of operating speeds of as fast as a billionth of a second, a single modern computer can process information fed to it simultaneously by literally hundreds of terminals, located virtually anywhere. All that is needed is the communications facility —the telephone line, the satellite network, the microwave network, or the cable—through which the data can move from the terminal to the computer and from the computer to the terminal. Some of these computers also allow batch processing to be conducted even while problems are being solved and data are being inputted and retrieved through different terminal devices.

Effectively, then, what the development and application of terminals has meant is the creation of a multifunctioning, multipurpose computer with many fingers. To visualize how this works, and the speed with which it operates, think of the back of your hand as the computer, each of your fingernails as a terminal, and each of your fingers as the transmission link connecting each terminal to the computer. By rapidly wiggling your fingers, you are duplicating the actions of input and output, with each terminal acting independently yet simultaneously with every other terminal. However, there is a very significant difference between this illustration and the actual use of computer terminals: certain communications devices can interact with different computers, simply by "dialing" the number of the required computer, whereas your fingernail terminals, permanently connected to your "back-of-the-hand" computer, can interact only with that one computer.

The rapidly increasing use of computer terminals during the past five years leaves little doubt that access to and use of the computer from remote distances will be the way of the future, and that the direction predominantly will be toward the individual and his personal information needs. Even now, virtually every home, office, factory, school, hospital—almost any institution you can name—has, in its

Every home, office, school, store or other facility has in the telephone the basic equipment needed to communicate with a computer. Push-button phones such as these can even input information to a computer directly through the keyboard.

telephone, the basic equipment for establishing a communications link with some computer. In fact, although the procedure is rather slow, push-button, touch-tone telephones can, with some modification, be used for directly inputting information to a computer by punching the digits on the telephone's keyboard.

Besides specially constructed TV and typewriter terminals, other types of terminals can be used for communicating with the computer. Pressure sensors beneath the street or electronic eyes beside a road, for instance, can note cars moving down all the streets in a city and transmit the information directly to a computer. The computer then can control the timing of traffic lights to allow the fastest movement of vehicles in all directions.

Sensors beneath the street also can communicate with a computer in an automobile. This could eventually allow a driver to move from one location to another in an unfamiliar city. The sensors would give the car-computer information about where the car is presently located in relation to where the driver wants to go. The computer then would determine the route by "reading" the sensors and would indicate by a dashboard signal each intersection at which the driver should turn.

Electronic monitoring instruments attached to the skin of a hospital patient can transmit information about his condition to a computer where the data are monitored. Should the computer note that something is wrong with the patient, it would immediately notify a hospital attendant and the patient's doctor.

Even household television sets can be adapted to transmit information to a computer via a telephone line, or cable connection. Although adapting the television set for use as a terminal would be costly, it would not affect the ability of the set to receive regular programs.

Actually, there is almost no limit to the types of terminals which can be developed and the ways in which they can be used. However, widespread access to and use of these terminals by the general public, except perhaps for selected purposes such as education, probably will not be realized until sometime toward the middle to late 1980's or even the early 1990's. Time is still needed to solve a number of problems, such as the insufficient supply of transmission facilities, the tremendous numbers of programs which need to be written, and the limited ability of present-day computers to handle absolutely mammoth data storage, retrieval and processing requirements.

Efforts to correct these situations, of course, already are under way. Greater numbers of vastly improved transmission facilities are constantly being developed. Witness, for example, the tremendous growth and use of satellite communications networks. Programming methods are becoming more and more simplified each day, thus increasing the speed with which programs can be developed.

Constant improvements are also being made in computers themselves. We will certainly see during the next few years further attempts to increase speed. Despite the fact that today's computer circuits react two and one-half million times faster than the human nerve cell, they still impose serious delays in the processing of certain jobs such as weather forecasting. Currently, the computer takes approximately half a day to process a 24-hour forecast. Ideally, it should take no longer than about one hour. Scientists believe that, to meet the requirements of the future, computers will have to operate five hundred to one thousand times faster than present equipment, or at speeds ranging around one trillion operations a second. And when an action is taken in a trillionth of a second, it is occurring in the equivalent fraction of time that one second is to all the seconds in slightly over 300 years.

These great speeds will possibly be accomplished through refinement of technologies already known. One approach involves the integration of highly complex electronic functions currently handled by different electronic components into a single component. This technique is known as large-scale integration, and results not only in higher computer speeds and lower power consumption, but also in a significant reduction in the cost of computer production.

Development of cryogenic memories is another approach which will increase speed as well as help expand the size of computer memories. Cryogenics, as applied to electronics, is the operation of electrical components and component connectors in a temperature environment of almost absolute zero, or about −459°F. This temperature produces a situation known as superconductivity—that is, the ability of some metals to conduct electricity with almost no resistance. In a non-cryogenic environment, the resistance of the metal in the conducting wires and components retards the movement of electrical pulses, causing the pulses to lose some of their power as they move from one point to another. In the extreme cold of absolute-zero temperatures, the resistance almost completely disappears, and so the pulses retain most of their strength and speed.

Pieces of thin photographic film coated with iron oxide may replace magnetic cores in tomorrow's computers. These films will make it possible to store far more information in far less space than magnetic cores now allow, resulting in smaller computers capable of handling vastly more data than present models. It is further possible that these thin-film computers may be operating in a cryogenic environment. Some scientists, in fact, believe the thin-film cryogenic computer memory may be available by the middle to late 1970's, once an economical way is found to provide the cooling needed to maintain a near absolute-zero temperature.

Other remarkable advances in computer technology will undoubtedly make use of the laser, the hologram and speech recognition.

Just about everyone, of course, has heard of the laser, although not everyone understands exactly what it is. Actually, the word *laser* is an acronym—that is, a word made up of the first letters of several words in a phrase. In this case, *laser* comes from the first letters of the words describing a scientific process known as *L*ight *A*mplification by *S*timulated *E*mission of *R*adiation. A laser produces a thin beam of light that, depending on its power output, can burn a hole in a diamond, carry the signals of many different TV pictures at one time, transmit information from point to point within a computer, or project a three-dimensional picture.

Laser light and ordinary light are quite different from

This ruby laser's energy is so intense it can bore a ⅟₁₆-inch hole in a sapphire in a thousandth of a second. Laser energy can be controlled so that the beam can transmit information from point to point within a computer.

each other. Ordinary light is *incoherent:* that is, it is made up of many different wavelengths that scatter out in different directions. Laser light, on the other hand, is *coherent;* it is made up of light of one wavelength which moves in one direction. Ordinary light from the sun or a light bulb, for example, is composed of many different wavelengths. Each wavelength represents a different color, and these different color wavelengths scatter out from the source in many different directions. By comparison, light from a laser has been made all one wavelength, or color, by passing it back and forth many times through a crystal, a gas or a liquid which screens out all but the wavelengths of one color. Furthermore, these identical wavelengths are "straightened" into parallel lines by the crystal, gas or liquid through which they pass, so that the waves are "in phase" with one another.

Scientists today have already developed a device called an optical converter which could be used in a computer to recognize and store information projected by the light from a laser. This converter could enable a computer to process data at a rate of 10 trillion alphabetic, numeric and special characters a second—10,000 times faster than is currently possible. Production of this computer at an economical cost, however, is at least a decade away, perhaps longer.

Somewhat closer in time is the *hologram,* a Greek word meaning "whole writing." A hologram is a piece of photographic film much like that used in conventional cameras but which is exposed by a laser beam rather than by ordinary light.

In producing a hologram, a low-power laser beam is aimed at a three-dimensional object, such as the model of a building. The light is reflected off the model, hits the photographic film and turns the grains of film emulsion light or dark in proportion to the highlights of the model. However, before the reflected laser beam reaches the film, it must pass through another beam of laser light which has been separated from the original laser beam and mirrored across the path of the reflected beam.

This reflected beam is broken up by the irregular surface of the model, and consequently, is "out of phase" with the unbroken mirrored beam. This step is what gives the hologram its three-dimensional image, for the out-of-phase beam now carries information about the lightness and darkness of the model, which is all you see in a conventional photograph, plus information about the precise distance of those light and dark areas from the film. You will not see the three-dimensional image by looking at the exposed holographic film under ordinary conditions, however. The image will appear only when laser light is projected through the exposed holographic film.

In the computer, plates of holographic film approximately 10 inches square register images that convey alphabetic, numeric and picture information. These plates of holographic film are subdivided into one-millimeter squares called "pages." (A millimeter is about $\frac{4}{100}$ of an inch.)

A holographic film, when a laser beam is focused on it, can store more than 100 million bits of information within nine square inches. This sample pattern, projected by a laser beam on a piece of ground glass, shows only a small portion of the information contained on the actual hologram.

Each page holds up to 10,000 bits of data, which can be recorded and retrieved for processing via a single burst of a laser beam.

At the present time, most research in lasers and holograms involves what is known as an argon laser. This is a laser which creates light by passing an electric current through argon gas. Scientists hope, however, that one day lasers of a different variety will be possible, lasers which will generate less heat and require less power to produce a beam than does argon gas equipment.

Speech and voice recognition, another computer innovation, will almost certainly be achieved by the early to middle 1970's. Even now, in fact, the technology is in the experimental stages.

Speech recognition means that the computer can accept verbal instructions inputted by telephone, microphone or any other audio-transmission device. Such instructions may then be applied by the computer to solve some problem, to direct some piece of machinery, to update or correct stored records, or even to answer a request for information. In the latter situation, the computer itself may respond verbally, a technique already possible.

Voice recognition means that the computer can determine who is speaking by matching the voice of the person speaking against a file of voices maintained within the computer. When characteristics of the spoken voice match the characteristics of a voice stored in the computer, the identity of the speaker is established. One of the several possible uses of voice recognition may be to verify that a person requesting computer records is authorized to receive them.

Speech and voice recognition are both accomplished by using a technique called *voice analysis*. This involves the development of a *voice print*, which like a fingerprint is characteristic of one person only. The voice print is produced by an analog computer, which then transmits a numerical description of the print to a digital computer. (An *analog computer* is different from a *digital computer* in that it measures information continuously, whereas a digital computer counts each unit of information separately. An automobile speedometer, for example, is a simple form of analog computer in that it continuously measures the speed at which the car is traveling. But a turnstile is a form of digital computer in that it separately counts the number of people moving past it. Because of the far greater number of digital computers in use today, the word "computer" always refers to a digital computer.)

In developing a "voice print," the analog computer measures different characteristics of the words being spoken. The voice print includes, in part, measurement of *pitch*, which is the number of vibrations per second of the vocal cords; measurement of *resonance*, which is the supplementary sound created by release of air through the throat, mouth and nasal passages; measurement of intensity of *"unvoiced" sounds* such as the "S" sound in "hiss," of the *"unvoiced fricatives"* (S, F, TH), of the *"voiced fricatives"* (Z, V), and of the *"plosives"* (P, T, B, D). Each measurement is numerically coded, and the code is transmitted to the digital computer, where it is translated into binary numbers. These binary numbers can be compared with the binary numbers standing for different words that have already been stored in the computer memory. When the stored words are spoken by specific persons, the computer can identify the speaker by comparing the voice characteristics of the spoken words (now in binary form) with those of the stored words (also in binary form). To determine *what* the person is saying, all the computer has to do is compare the spoken words against a stored vocabulary of words. The computer then acts on the spoken words by following a set of stored program instructions which tell it exactly what steps to take for each word received. If, for instance, a person says, "Give me the titles of all novels written by Ernest Hemingway," program instructions would tell the computer to take these actions on the words "give me," "titles," "novels," and "Ernest Hemingway":

"Give me"—provide the requesting party with information.

"Titles"—select peripheral memory device containing information on all works having titles.

"Novels"—select the area of the peripheral memory device containing titles of novels.

"Ernest Hemingway"—select the area of the peripheral memory device containing titles of novels written by Ernest Hemingway.

In programming a computer so that jobs like this can be done, action on the words "Give me" would be taken last, for only when the requested information had been selected could it be provided to the party needing it. Also, the programming steps would be far more complex than the ones presented in this illustration, for besides telling the computer what to do, they would also have to tell how to do it and in what order each step was to be taken.

In computers that are currently tailored for speech and voice recognition, only a limited number of words can be recognized, primarily because of limitations in the size of the memory units and in the speed of the computers themselves. Furthermore, programming can be quite difficult because of the almost infinite number of word combinations which can be used. However, as large-memory, high-speed computers such as laser-hologram systems become available, computer-stored vocabularies as extensive as one thousand to twenty thousand or more words may be possible.

These new developments of computer technology, as well as others which might be developed, make it possible to envision the not-too-distant appearance of computers operating at speeds measurable in trillionths of a second, capable of recording trillions of bits of information, and geared for simultaneous communication with hundreds or perhaps thousands of terminals situated anywhere around the world. Furthermore, these terminals will allow transmission of data of different forms to the computer, and retrieval of information from the computer in the same form or in a different form from the way the original information was presented.

To some, these possibilities may sound like science fiction. But it will happen and is happening even now. Less than fifteen years ago the Russians propelled the first rocket into outer space; today man stands on the moon. The same pace of advancement applies to the development of computers.

What does all this mean for man? It is hard to say, for only as man becomes personally involved with the computer will he begin to realize its effect on his life and his way of living. By recognizing certain of these involvements now, he can at least better prepare himself for the future.

IV / Teacher, Teacher: Who's the Teacher?

Much that man does starts with education. Thus it is not unusual that the classroom already is witnessing some of the computer advances anticipated for the next quarter century.

Currently, almost all educational institutions are using computers to handle their accounting, to prepare classroom schedules, and to perform other administrative chores. Some also are using the computer for student instruction. However, these are mostly the colleges and universities that use it primarily for the batch processing of problems that have been coded on punched cards and submitted by engineering, science and business administration students. Certain school systems also have set up computer-based education networks on a citywide or countywide level designed to teach large numbers of pupils simultaneously yet on an individual basis. In New York City, for example, a single computer currently provides reading, mathematics and spelling lessons to some 6,000 elementary-grade students situated in sixteen different schools throughout the city. Over 200 children can take these lessons at the same time, using computer-communications terminals located within the sixteen schools.

The computer used in New York City is not a time-sharing computer, however; students cannot input new data to the computer or have that data processed according to their own instructions. The students can only respond to information transmitted from the computer and presented on their terminals.

So far, only a few schools (and even fewer school systems) have installed time-sharing computers. But the number of schools and school systems considering their use is increasing. Movement in this direction, coupled with activities already taking place in computer instruction, thus gives some idea of what education may be like in the future.

First of all, the appearance of tomorrow's classrooms could change considerably. Rather than sitting at rows of desks or tables listening to a teacher, elementary and high school students may sit at TV and typewriter terminals facing a central console. This console, connected to the school's computer, or the school system's computer, would contain a special keyboard and television screen operated by the teacher. By typing instructions on the console keyboard, the teacher could cause the computer to display either the same or different study-information at any or all of the student terminals. Spoken words describing what the students are viewing might also be provided by the computer through a set of headphones which each student has placed over his ears.

Noise in this classroom would be at a minimum, for each student would be concentrating on the information presented at his terminal. When the terminal presented a question, the student would answer it by punching one or more keys on his keyboard. He might also take his exams on this terminal, with the computer doing the grading and telling the student when he has made a mistake. The student then could correct his mistake while the problem was still fresh in his mind . . . although the correction would not change his grade on the exam.

Today's school children learn more and faster when they use terminals such as these for individualized computer instruction. Schools of tomorrow may see all students taught in this manner.

Using the terminal would not eliminate a student's contact with the teacher, however. If the student required assistance, either with the operation of the terminal or with the meaning of the information, he could inform the teacher by pushing a special number key on his terminal. The teacher could then come to the student's terminal and help him, or she could have the subject he was studying displayed on her TV screen and discuss the problem with the student through a telephone connection at his terminal. Students who are at home ill may also be able to continue their school work by using bedside terminals connected by phone line to the teacher's console.

In this type of classroom, tomorrow's elementary and high school students probably will learn more in two years of school than today's students learn in three, partly because the computer will make possible more individual instruction, and partly because there will be so much more to learn. In the lower elementary grades, the use of the terminals probably will involve nothing more than responding to information called forth from the computer by the teacher and displayed on the student's television screen. This information could be in alphabetical and numerical form, or in the form of drawings, or even films which the computer, in response to its programming, would select from a library of cartridge films which it manages. Not until the fourth or possibly fifth year of school, however, might the student be given the opportunity to guide the actions of the computer from his terminal, for he will first have to learn certain basics of computer operation, and perhaps even of computer programming.

Because of computer-assisted instruction, some educators believe the day could come when many subjects will be taught outside the classroom. Most likely, this sort of instruction would be found chiefly at the college and university levels, or, to a lesser extent, at the high school level. It is unlikely, however, that course instruction outside the classroom could be attempted at the elementary-school level, since grade-school children probably would not have sufficient self-motivation to study without supervision.

Courses offered outside the classroom probably would be taken by students using computer terminals situated in soundproof alcoves, or "carrels" as they are called, in buildings on the campus. These carrels would be available to all students for study or research, and would enable the student to participate in a course at his own rate of learning. Subject material would be provided to the student identifying himself to the computer by voice or number as being registered for a particular course. Examinations would be taken through the carrel terminal, too, and the computer would record the results. For quizzes and other periodic tests, the student might be given his grade on the terminal as soon as he completed the test. A printed grade also might be provided to the course instructor. But for final examinations, test results probably would be given only to the instructor, who would then determine the final grade for the course.

College courses provided by computer might also enable students to enjoy a study schedule far more flexible than present-day classrooms offer. If a student, on a given day, wanted to study the material offered in one course for five hours and the material offered in another course for only half an hour, that would be his prerogative. If he wanted to work during the day and study at night, he could do that. And if he didn't want to study at all, that, too, could be his choice, although the computer might eliminate him from the course if he didn't maintain at least a minimum level of progress.

Although there is no assurance that this country will turn to an all-encompassing system of instruction by computer, a strong possibility nonetheless does exist. The major consideration at this time, though, is not whether such an educational system will be developed, but what it might mean if it should be.

First of all, what about the teacher? Will the teacher become less important or less necessary in an educational system using the computer? The answer is: Probably not. Teachers are likely to be just as important and necessary as they are today. But their basic responsibility may change, for they will be dealing with new ways in which subject material is presented to and learned by each student.

One of these new ways is known as *programmed learning*. This is the development of special educational packages covering selected aspects of a particular subject. For example, separate educational packages can be made up for the principles of binary arithmetic; for adding, subtracting, multiplying and dividing binary numbers; and for the applications of binary numbers. When these units are presented in consecutive order, they provide a progressive means of helping the student understand binary numbers.

The information contained in each of these educational packages is structured, or "programmed," in such a way that the student is "guided" through the subject material; that is, he is taken step by step from the most basic and elementary information through the most complex information which can be presented at his particular grade level. Furthermore, each new piece of information is usually related to some previous piece of information, so as to help the student understand its meaning more easily.

Just as important as the programmed package itself is the way the information it contains is presented. Many of today's programmed-learning packages are tailored for use in special teaching machines. Programmed-learning information that has been recorded on photographic slides can, for instance, be displayed on a desk-top instrument having a small slide-projection screen and a keyboard. After a student has viewed the information displayed on the screen, he can push a keyboard button and cause the next slide to appear automatically. In many programmed-learning packages, certain slides contain questions for the student to answer. He answers by pressing the button (or buttons) on the keyboard that he feels represents the correct answer to the question. If the answer is correct, the instrument is automatically advanced to the next slide. However, if the answer is not correct, a slide containing the information to which the question refers may be automatically redisplayed on the screen before the question appears for the student to answer again.

Every day, more and more educators, and even some businessmen, are becoming involved in developing these programmed-learning packages. Many persons also are becoming increasingly involved in developing whole "programmed" school curricula using textbooks based on the programmed-learning concept.

Up to now, the teacher has been primarily responsible for guiding a classroomful of students through the maze of information contained in textbooks, lectures and audio-visual presentations. However, greater use of programmed-learning methods may greatly reduce this responsibility. And if programmed-learning subjects are stored within a computer, the teacher's responsibility may be reduced even further.

Obviously, the teacher would have to learn how to use programmed-learning procedures and how to operate the computer. Also, the teacher would have to learn to recognize, by test scores, a student who was not responding quickly enough to certain material. He would then have to decide whether the material should be changed or simplified or whether the student should just review the programmed material he has already studied. Similarly, the teacher would have to learn to recognize the student who was progressing rapidly through the programs and make available to him advanced material which might originally have been scheduled for a later date.

Effectively, then, tomorrow's teacher will be teaching his students on a far more individual basis than he does today. Furthermore, if programmed learning allows students to progress at their own rate, it may no longer be necessary or even possible to separate students into grades. The teacher would then have to guide learning activities not just on one grade level at a time but on all grade levels simultaneously. Indeed, it is very likely that the elementary-school teacher might ultimately specialize in just one subject (mathematics, for example) for all grades, just as the high school and college instructor now do.

Education of teachers, too, might change from the present four-year college program, followed by refresher courses, to a program of continuous training. In fact, the education of all people, regardless of age or employment position, may have to become continuous, simply to stay abreast of new information. This ongoing education might be secured in the home, using nothing more than a computer terminal. Course content might be provided free of charge—as National Educational Television courses are provided today—or a small tuition fee might be added to the telephone bill.

It is also possible to foresee the day when academic degrees become a thing of the past and people are evaluated for jobs solely on their ability rather than on the number of years they have spent in school. Thus, a highly intelligent and diligent high school graduate might be considered as qualified for a particular job as a college graduate, or a two-year college student just as qualified as a six-year college student.

This new educational plan could enable a student to serve as an apprentice on a job and find out whether he is suited for it before he makes the heavy financial commitment of a college training program in a particular field. It might also help the person who can't afford a formal college education to obtain an equivalent education by using computer terminals in his home or office which can be connected by phone line to a university's computer.

Will all these changes in the present pattern of education actually take place during the final decades of the 20th century? It is possible. Maybe it's even beginning to happen in some school near you right now.

V

I, The Machine, Accuse

Not long ago a man arrested for disorderly conduct in a New Orleans tavern was taken to a local police station for booking. His name and description were immediately tele-typed to the FBI National Crime Information Center in Washington, D.C., where the information was checked against a file containing identifications of persons wanted by the police anywhere in the nation. Seconds later, even before the desk sergeant in New Orleans could record the charge against the arrested man, a reply from Washington was re-ceived: The man was wanted for murder in California.

Only because of the rapid interaction between the New Orleans police and the FBI was this criminal apprehended. And only because the National Crime Information Center had the relevant information stored within a computer where it was instantly accessible to police officials in New Orleans was it possible to determine in seconds that the person was "wanted." Otherwise, the man might have been held a short time, brought before a magistrate on the disorderly conduct charge, fined perhaps five dollars, and then released; by the time the police could have referred his fingerprints to the

FBI for identification, the man could have been anywhere in the nation.

Significant? Indeed it is, for today the National Crime Information Center in Washington forms the hub of an ever expanding law enforcement computer and communications network blanketing the entire fifty states of the union. Ten or fifteen years from now the electronic umbrella may be so complete that even you might be scrutinized by some computer—should you attempt to commit a crime.

Most people probably have a general idea of the meaning of the word *crime,* but few realize what a really broad word it is. Nor do many realize how difficult it can sometimes be to determine who a criminal suspect might be, or where he might be located.

Crimes, first of all, are those acts of human behavior prohibited by law which carry the possibility of conviction and punishment to persons engaged in them. Any unlawful act, no matter how minor, is therefore a crime. Secondly, in this age of rapid mobility, crime knows no geographical boundaries. For this reason, it may be extremely difficult to apprehend a criminal suspect, even when his identity is known; within five hours by plane or four to five days by car, a person can travel from New York to California or any other point in the nation, leaving the scene of a crime far behind him.

Because of the National Crime Information Center and its extensive, up-to-the-minute computer files, movement of criminals between states is becoming more difficult. In Phoenix, Arizona, for instance, a policeman stopped a car for endangering the lives of pedestrians walking through a crosswalk and questioned the driver. Since the driver's answers seemed suspicious, the policeman stepped to a nearby call box and contacted his precinct station. Within moments he was informed that the car had been stolen in Chicago and that the driver was wanted for a supermarket robbery in St. Louis; the information had been retrieved by teletype directly from the National Crime Information Center's computer in Washington.

In California, a State Police officer stopped a car that was pulling another car. Everything looked normal until the officer radioed his headquarters for information on the two cars and on the driver and the driver's companion. Within moments, the word came back: The car being pulled had been stolen in Nevada; the car being driven had been stolen in Los Angeles; the driver was wanted in California for jumping bail; and the driver's companion was wanted in Texas for illegal possession of narcotics. Again, the information was provided by the National Crime Information Center's computer.

On the Ohio Turnpike, a State Trooper chased a speeding car. Even while the trooper was in pursuit, he radioed his headquarters for a vehicle identification. Twenty seconds later he received this reply: "Registered owner of vehicle wanted in Indiana and may be armed. Proceed with caution." When the trooper stopped the car, he did so with revolver drawn. His search of the driver showed that the driver was indeed armed. Without the National Crime Information Center's computer, the trooper might have been wounded or perhaps even killed.

Using computers in this way to isolate and identify criminal suspects could lead to the day when it will be virtually impossible for any criminal to avoid being detected and apprehended. The National Crime Information Center is a step in that direction. An even more important step toward that goal is the development of law enforcement computer-communications systems on the local and statewide level, many of which even now are operating or are being installed.

In Kansas City, Missouri, for example, a computerized information retrieval system allows patrolmen to investigate as many as twenty-five reports of stolen or missing vehicles in the same amount of time it previously took to investigate just one; all the stolen-vehicle information is recorded in a

Law enforcement agencies throughout the nation are now install-
ing computer systems for crime control. Eventually these systems
will be linked together, with terminals used to identify vehicle
registrations, stolen cars and other stolen property, guns and
wanted persons anywhere in the nation.

computer the instant it is received, rather than written by
hand on forms which will later be distributed. Also, the
system can instantly provide information on the arrest and
conviction records, fingerprint codes, and aliases of wanted
persons, and can directly transmit this information to and
retrieve it from the National Crime Information Center in
Washington.

In Cincinnati, Ohio, another law enforcement computer
and communications system enables city and county police
officials to obtain via teletype or TV terminal information
on stolen vehicles, wanted persons, guns and stolen property.
Criminal records, stored in the same computer, can also be
obtained in seconds by using these terminals, as can Motor

Vehicle Department records, vehicle inspection records, and court records maintained in other government agency computers. Furthermore, the Cincinnati law enforcement computer is linked directly by communications lines to the National Crime Information Center, to computers used by the Ohio Highway Patrol, and to police and government agency computers in Kentucky, just across the Ohio River.

Possibly the most advanced local computer and communications system, however, is the one recently installed in California. This system is a network of communications lines, all under computer control, which crisscross the state and enable different police agencies to input information to and retrieve information from computers belonging to different state law enforcement agencies and to communicate with the National Crime Information Center. The result is instant information, whenever and wherever it is needed—information which previously was difficult to obtain.

Here is an example of how the law enforcement computer-communications system in California might work sometime in the future:

Imagine that it is around 8:45 A.M. on a Saturday morning, and the owner of a Los Angeles men's clothing store has just reported to the police that his shop had been robbed sometime during the previous evening or early morning. When an investigation of the store, including a check for fingerprints, produces no results, the officer assigned to the case calls his headquarters and gives the officer on duty a list of the stolen merchandise and a description of the method used to enter the store—the "modus operandi," or MO.

Immediately, the officer on duty sits down at a teletype and transmits the MO information to a Los Angeles County law enforcement computer for comparison against MO information stored inside it. Then, using the same teletype, he transmits the list of stolen merchandise to another law enforcement computer in California and to the National Crime Information Center in Washington. Both actions are completed in less than two minutes.

Hardly has the officer finished transmitting information on the stolen property when his teletype begins printing a response to his MO inquiry. This is a listing of people known or believed to be residing in Los Angeles and the surrounding areas who have been selected from California and National Crime Information Center computer files on the basis of such information as:

> previous robberies having the same MO, for which the listed person has been convicted and served a sentence; previous robberies where he has been a suspect and not convicted, but where the earlier MO matches the present MO;
> and robberies for which each listed person previously has been convicted, or apprehended and subsequently released, in which burglary of a clothing store was involved.

Furthermore, these files have provided the communicating officer with a complete description of each suspect; where each is now presumed to be located; and the model and license number of the car each may own and may be driving.

The officer on duty now transmits, by teletype, everything but the MO information as part of a wanted-person bulletin to all law enforcement agencies in California. And each of these agencies in turn radios the information to the patrol cars operating in its jurisdiction. Probably no more than thirty minutes have elapsed since the moment the investigator first contacted the officer on duty.

Now the search for the suspects begins, not only in Los Angeles but throughout the state. The point to remember, however, is not so much the speed with which these suspects may be located, although this is important, but rather the speed with which the suspects are selected; the speed with which a communiqué of their descriptions and a list of the stolen merchandise is transmitted to all California law enforcement agencies; and the speed with which a listing of the stolen property is transmitted for recording at the National Crime Information Center.

Of course, none of the suspects selected by the computer may have been involved in the clothing store robbery, as further investigation may show. But the odds do favor the possibility that one of them was involved, for most criminals who have gotten away with one crime will attempt to repeat their success with a similar crime. Even the first-time thief who has no criminal record in computer files in California or in Washington, D.C., or the thief residing outside California will not find it easy to avoid being detected and apprehended, for sooner or later he will probably attempt to dispose of the stolen property. And when he makes such an attempt, whether in California or in some other state, he immediately jeopardizes his seclusion, since any legitimate retailer or other potential buyer of the merchandise who suspects that it may be stolen can have the police run an immediate check on the property through California and National Crime Information Center computer files.

Fast as these law enforcement computers are in recording and retrieving information on crime, one problem still remains. This is the need for police officers in the field to radio or telephone requests for information to an officer on duty at a precinct station or headquarters, who then must relay the request to a computer. In other words, the officer in the field cannot at the present time directly communicate with the computer; when several officers all need information at the same time, delay can become critical.

In the near future, however, this problem may be solved. Several law enforcement agencies throughout the nation are right now testing the use of small keyboard terminals attached to patrol car dashboards for direct computer-communication. Also, with the perfection of voice-recognition procedures, an officer should eventually be able to talk directly to the computer, either by telephone or by radio.

So far, most of the information stored within the different city and state law enforcement computers and within the National Crime Information Center computers relates to robberies, murders, assaults, traffic in narcotics, illegal gambling, etc.—the serious crimes known as felonies. But what about information relating to traffic violations, petty thefts, shoplifting, vandalism, etc.—the lesser crimes known as misdemeanors?

In most states now almost all information about driver's licenses, motor vehicle registrations and motor vehicle violations are stored within a computer. By using this computer, a police officer can readily determine, before he makes an arrest, whether a car violating a motor vehicle law is stolen. And once he has made the arrest, he can determine, through the same communications network, whether the vehicle registration is valid, whether the license of the driver is valid, and what history of violation the driver has. Consequently, the patrolman can better decide whether to hold the driver or to issue a summons and release him.

Ultimately, a police officer may not even have to be present to identify a speeding vehicle. Identification will be made by installing optical scanning devices at intervals in or alongside a road. Numbers embossed on the bottom of the car frame or on the side of the car would be read automatically as the car passed over or by the optical device— even if the car was moving at 100 miles per hour—and the data would be transmitted directly to a computer. This computer would be able to identify the car which was speeding, calculate how fast the car was traveling in excess of the posted speed limit, determine the owner of the vehicle (though not necessarily its driver), and print and mail a summons. Furthermore, by installing such optical scanners in or alongside all major national roads, the police could determine the whereabouts of any vehicle moving almost anywhere within the country.

Information about persons involved in other types of misdemeanors even now is being recorded in some cities and states in computers operated and maintained by various branches of the judiciary and by certain social service agencies. So far, the amount of data recorded in these computers is limited. However, most law enforcement officials believe that the magnitude and the scope of this information will increase, and that someday such data will become part of the crime information records now available through the computer-communications networks of city, state and national law enforcement agencies. Also, it is reasonable to expect that the different state agencies involved in the prosecution of crime, such as the district attorney's office and the judiciary, and the agencies involved in the rehabilitation of convicted criminals, such as the penal institutions and parole boards, may be added to the network, too, thus enabling them to deal more efficiently—and more effectively—with the cases they are handling.

As these different facets of the crime information network are put together, law enforcement officials believe it will be possible to eliminate much of the crime prevailing today. Some persons, however, oppose using the computer for law enforcement, fearing it might become a "watchdog" of all human activities, criminal and otherwise. This possibility, of course, does exist, and must be controlled by the selection of responsible public officials by concerned citizens. Certainly the information storage capacity of the computer is, or soon will be, more than adequate to maintain volumes of personal information. Moreover, voice recognition could identify people speaking during telephone or radio conversations, and recording pictures of faces in computer memory could make possible rapid identification through TV monitoring.

Let us hope, though, that such a time of universal surveillance will never come. According to the FBI, the "full capability" of a computerized crime information system will be achieved—and will end—"on the day when wanted men are at an absolute minimum, and when their pictures in the post office are there strictly for decorative purposes."

VI

Where, Oh Where
Did the Money Go?

Imagine living in a nation where no one uses money, yet where merchandise and services are bought and sold just as if money existed.

Sounds unlikely, doesn't it? But it is possible, right now, right here in this country.

Bankers call this sort of living the "cashless society," and while most of them will not admit its day is near, they won't deny it, either. However, they will tell you why it is needed.

The reason is paper, too much paper. Under our present methods of doing business, almost every purchase or financial transaction is accompanied by slips of paper: currency, checks, money orders, receipts, invoices, bills, ledgers, credit memos, and so forth. As the population grows, as the production of goods and services increases, as the amount of money people earn and spend rises, the day draws closer when the entire economy of the nation may be brought to a standstill, buried beneath a mountain of paper.

Dr. James Hiller, president of a well-known research laboratory, describes the situation as "The Tyranny of Numbers Versus the Constancy of Humans." By this phrase Dr.

Hiller means that a bank teller, a store clerk, a stock broker, an accountant, a credit clerk—anyone involved in the counting of or accounting for money—can handle only so many slips of paper in a given working day. But the number of financial transactions, and thus the number of pieces of paper, which must be handled is increasing at a rate faster than that of the population. Soon there may not be enough people in the world to handle just the paper generated by the buying, selling and billing in this country.

Historically, whenever the "tyranny of numbers" has begun to outrun the "constancy of humans," man has sought and usually found some technological solution. When the volume of telephone calls began exceeding the ability of human operators to route them, man developed and eventually implemented direct dialing and computerized switching. When the amount of mail some years ago became more than postal employees could efficiently handle, zip codes were introduced as a prelude to full-scale mechanization of post-office functions, something not yet possible but now very close to realization.

Now that the number and complexity of financial transactions is creating serious paper-handling problems within the stock market and is seriously threatening the banking industry, it seems reasonable that the introduction of "mechanized money," and the appearance of the "cashless society," could be just around the corner. Indeed, there is considerable evidence that the nation even now is turning to an economy where there will be no money, particularly no folding money (currency) or slips of paper used to represent money (checks and money orders).

Consider, first of all, the credit card activity of banks alone. In 1965, there were fewer than five million bank credit cards in circulation, most of them issued in California by Bank of America. Today, there are nearly fifty million bank credit cards in circulation, issued by nearly 8,000 banks throughout the nation. Furthermore, in 1969 the amount of consumer borrowing by bank card exceeded 2 billion dollars—up seventy percent over 1968. Although this figure represents only two percent of the approximately 120 billion dollars borrowed by consumers that year, bank officials believe that within a decade over twenty-five percent of all consumer borrowing will be handled by bank credit cards.

Karl Hinke, chairman of Interbank Card Association, a cooperative credit card network, says that "we could call the establishment of the bank charge card a new medium of exchange, a renaissance of banking. The credit card of the future will be a membership card in a nationwide— eventually international—electronic payment and book-keeping network. It has the potential of eliminating many conventional uses of checks and money."

Next, consider that most of the nation's major retail stores also have their own credit card plans; that almost all airlines and gasoline companies have theirs; that there are several different companies providing credit cards for entertainment (American Express, Diners Club, Carte Blanche); and that even some supermarkets have initiated their own credit card programs.

What is the reason for this rapid proliferation of credit card programs? First of all, a credit card is nothing more than an embossed piece of plastic which identifies a person's credit reliability; that is, his ability to pay. The amount of credit he is entitled to is based on his earnings and his past reliability in paying what he owes. When a person hands a credit card to a merchant, it is like saying, "I am buying this product or service now, even though I may or may not have the money to pay for it at this time. However, with this card I do guarantee payment in full when you send me a bill, either immediately following receipt of the bill or as a series of smaller payments extended over a period of months." Buying on credit, or "on time" as it is called when payment is spread over a period of months, stimulates the nation's economy by keeping money in constant circulation rather than tied up in banks, cookie jars or mattresses until enough of it is accumulated for an immediate cash purchase.

Secondly, by providing credit and issuing credit cards, banks and stores earn considerable amounts of money; Bank of America, for example, netted 10 million dollars in the first ten months of 1969 just from its card operations in California alone. With most credit card plans, the credit card buyer is billed once a month for his purchases. The billing is handled either by the store, if the buyer has used the store's credit card, or by a bank, if the buyer has used a bank's credit card which the store has honored. In both cases, when the buyer extends payment of the bill over several months, he pays interest on the unpaid balance as of the end of each month. This interest can range from one to one and one-half percent a month, or up to eighteen percent a year, depending on state laws regulating the maximum amount of interest which can be charged. A $400 refrigerator thus can cost the credit buyer as much as $472 when he pays for it in twelve monthly installments. When a retail store has its own credit card program, it receives these additional interest earnings. When a bank provides credit on behalf of the store, though, the bank receives the additional earnings, plus about five percent of the price of the merchandise or service purchased, which the store pays to the bank.

While credit buying and the use of credit cards does not effectively reduce the paperwork problem at this time because there is still need for billing and accounting, ultimately it could eliminate the problem completely, simply by using credit cards in place of currency, checks and money orders and handling *all* financial accounting with an interacting, nationwide network of computers and computer terminals. First, however, there will have to be general acceptance by the public of credit and credit cards as an economic procedure. Then some central means of complete credit veri-

Currency, checks and money orders may be heading for extinction, to be replaced by credit cards which can be read by terminals connected directly to bank computers. TV-like terminals in every home will be used to keep track of earnings and expenditures in the "cashless society."

fication and control, covering all people in all parts of the country at all times, will have to be established. Finally, it will be necessary to have computer terminals in every home so that people can always know the status of their bank accounts.

Based on the current rate and number of credit card distribution, even to the extent of mailing cards to persons who have not requested them, it is obvious that the population is being given every opportunity to familiarize itself with credit card procedures. Also, a nationwide complex of computerized credit verification centers is being constructed whose sole responsibility is to indicate who is and who is not a good credit risk. Presently, it is extremely difficult to restrict the use of credit cards which are stolen, and to guard against issuing cards to persons who are slow in paying or who fail to pay their bills. This is particularly true of credit cards which are honored nationally and internationally, but it is also true to a lesser extent of cards which are honored only in local areas. With the construction of a nationwide complex of computerized credit verification centers, however, it could be made almost impossible for a person to use a stolen credit card or to continue purchasing merchandise while owing more than acceptable amounts on previous purchases. Whenever a card is presented to a store or bank clerk, a terminal at the counter could read and transmit the card identification number, and the amount of purchase, all of which has been entered on an attached keyboard, to the computer of the nearest credit verification center. This computer could then inform the clerk, by signal to the terminal, whether the card was acceptable. It could tell whether the card was a stolen one by comparing the number against a stored list of all stolen credit card numbers; or whether the card's owner was a poor credit risk by comparing the number against a stored list of credit card numbers indicating that the holder had exceeded authorized credit limits. Such "control" information, stored within every credit verification center computer in the country, could be updated continuously as new data was fed into the network by banks, stores, and other concerns providing or participating in credit card programs.

Beyond the proliferation of credit cards and the development of a nationwide network of credit verification centers, other developments also point to the coming of a "cashless society." One of these is the relatively recent—and already growing—procedure of depositing an employee's paycheck directly into his bank account rather than issuing a paycheck to the employee which he cashes and deposits. This direct transfer of earnings from company bank accounts to employee bank accounts probably will be a major part of "cashless society" operation.

Coupled with this procedure is bank payment of a customer's bills directly from his bank account. Many mortgage and time payments are now handled in this way, and in some areas of the country, persons can authorize their banks to pay utility bills, which are mailed, without the customer's even seeing them, directly to the bank, which deducts the amount from the customer's account. Ultimately, direct bank payment of *all* customer bills may become part of a "cashless society," primarily because it reduces paper handling tremendously. For example, in order to pay a utility company, a bank need only total the amounts owed to the utility company by the several thousand customers who use the bank and write only one check for this amount. The bank then deducts from each customer's account the part of the total figure which he owes.

Another step, which will even eliminate the printing of customer bills, may be the use of an automatic utility meter-reading system, a device now in the testing stages. This technique enables the computer of a utility company to "read" customer meters directly by public telephone lines each month and to prepare bills from these readings. Eventually, these bills may be paid automatically by tying the utility company's computer to the bank's computer, thus eliminating the need for monthly customer statements.

Still another development is the growing interest within the stock market in turning all buy-and-sell operations over to computers. Eventually, this computer procedure could lead to the elimination of stock certificates by simply maintaining ownership information within brokerage house computers. Even now there are some special brokerage firms preparing for this type of operation.

Finally, there is the development, perhaps only temporary, of companies geared to protect consumers against lost or stolen credit cards. For a fee of five dollars a year, one of these companies claims that within thirty seconds of being notified that a subscriber's credit cards have been lost or stolen, it can put a computer to work to detail the cards the subscriber owns and to notify the issuers of those cards that they are missing and that credit privileges should be cancelled.

When the "cashless society" is fully implemented, however, services of this type probably will not be needed. By that time credit cards should be constructed so that they will be unusable by anyone other than the authorized owner. Even now a company in California is marketing a money-dispensing machine which accepts credit cards that are almost impossible to forge.

This machine makes cash available to a bank's customers at any hour of the day or night. If a customer is approved for credit totaling $300, he receives six cards, each good for $50. If he needs cash late Saturday night when the bank is closed, he goes to the machine at the bank and puts one of the cards into a slot. Out comes an envelope with $50 in cash. If he needs more than $50, he continues feeding cards to the machine until the amount he requires is obtained or until he is out of cards.

The cards themselves are made up of two types of plastic laminated together with the customer's code between the sheets of plastic. This construction is what makes the cards almost impossible to counterfeit. If a customer loses his cards, he notifies the bank immediately. The bank then programs the machine so that when a stolen or lost card is inserted, the card is taken away and the person inserting the card is signaled to call the bank. No money comes out.

The problem with this type of credit card is that it is not universal; that is, it can be "read" only by machines constructed and programmed to read it, and such machines are quite expensive. For a truly universal card, one which can be read by all types of machines, which cannot be counterfeited, and which immediately identifies the owner, some form of holographic credit card may be used.

Various experimental models of this type of card already exist. One of these is a plastic card which contains a tiny holographic picture of the owner plus a coded number identifying the credit account. To the eye this holograph picture appears as a blank piece of film, but when the hologram is placed in a laser beam projector, the person's image and his account number immediately appear. This laser beam projector can be built into a relatively inexpensive computer terminal at a fairly low cost.

Forgery of holograph cards is extremely difficult, since the cost of developing a single card or even several hundred cards is just too high. However, when they are produced for the total population, the cost per card is well within reason. Using stolen holograph cards also is impossible, because each one bears a picture of the authorized owner which cannot be replaced or altered without destroying the entire card.

If the "cashless society" does become a reality, what might it mean to the people of the nation?

First, it will probably mean an empty wallet—empty, that is, of currency, checks, and money orders. About all a wallet will contain is a single credit card, a handful of change for purchasing items costing less than a dollar, and a stack of receipts.

The "cashless society" also might mean the end of trips to the bank—withdrawing cash for a night on the town, depositing enough money to cover a check written yesterday, or cashing a paycheck. Banks as we know them now may very likely disappear.

Finally, the "cashless society" may mean the end of monthly bills and statements. Utility bills, mortgage payments and credit payments probably will be automatically deducted, by bank computer, from a customer's account and credited to the accounts of those firms to which payment is owed. Similarly, throughout the week the person will use his one credit card to make all food, entertainment, gasoline, clothing and other purchases. The cost of these items will be deducted automatically from the buyer's bank account and credited to the seller's account. For merchandise which costs less than a dollar, customers will be able to obtain nickels, dimes and quarters from automatic change machines activated by the same credit card.

In total, then, the "cashless society" will eliminate currency and the various forms of paper representing currency, and substitute electronic pulses in a nationwide network of computer memories. To pay for groceries or any other merchandise costing more than a dollar, the person will simply hand the merchant his credit card, and the merchant will insert it in a counter-top terminal. After verifying the owner's identity by comparing the holograph image with the person, the merchant will total the amount of merchandise purchased, using a keyboard attached to the terminal, and then push a button. Immediately, the amount will be automatically transmitted to the bank identified by the account number on the buyer's card. The buyer's account will be debited by this amount and the seller's account credited.

At first glance it may appear that anyone could buy anything at any time regardless of the funds he might have on deposit at his bank. But this will be impossible, for when a person doing business with a local merchant overdraws his account, the merchant's terminal will immediately signal that payment is not possible. In some cases when an account is overdrawn, the bank might advance the required funds— if the person has previously agreed to pay the interest charge involved. This credit arrangement on overdrawn checking accounts can be made today with many banks.

For persons living in one section of the country and using a nationally recognized credit card in some other part of the country, transfer of funds will be much the same as it is today when checks are used. The store will transmit the transaction data from its terminal to the credit verification center computer, and that computer will relay the information to the bank of the customer. This bank, in turn, will debit the customer's account and transfer funds to the store's bank. In the case where a buyer wishes to pay for a purchase over a period of months, his bank will be notified of this by the store, and no payment or only a down payment will be deducted immediately from the buyer's account. However, the store will be paid in full by the buyer's bank.

With TV-like terminals in every home, a person will be able to query a bank computer at any time to determine the current financial status of his own or his family's account. Children twelve years and older could have their own cards for the family account, and their parents would then keep track of how much the children were spending and on what. For smaller children, allowances would be issued in change.

Bank records could be protected from the spying eyes of others by having the inquiring party identify himself to the computer by voice recognition. Access to records would be withheld if the characteristics of the transmitted voice did not match the voice print maintained by the computer as part of an individual's financial records.

Besides solving the paper-work crisis, the "cashless society" might make the life of the average man much easier, for he will be using a computer to keep track of all his financial transactions. At the same time, it might also make his life more complicated, for the opportunity for credit buying will be greater, and credit buying can be dangerous; the monthly payments might exceed the person's income. However, placing maximum credit limits on an individual's account should eliminate this possibility. A study carried out in 1968 by the Federal Reserve Board on bank credit cards states that "as cardholders gain experience . . . they will learn to manage [credit cards] to suit their needs just as they have learned to manage other forms of consumer credit."

Another danger of the "cashless society" is its threat to a

person's right to privacy, for all income and expenditure information will be recorded in one computer. However, having this information on hand may also help to correct certain national ills.

First of all, analyzing the earnings and expenditures of all citizens by computer could aid in the development of national economic programs better geared to control periods of inflation and recession.

Second, information available from "cashless society" records could help pinpoint employment trends, and lead to a better utilization of national manpower.

Last and possibly most important, a "cashless society" could have a profound effect on crime, including such borderline cases as tax evasion and questionable business practices. What national or international crime syndicate, for example, will want to import narcotics into this country when the buyer can provide only a credit card in payment? Certainly, the person selling the narcotics, or even the person buying them, will not want the amount of the transaction recorded on his financial records; tracing would be too easy. Even if the narcotics buyer gave the seller a stolen television set or other stolen merchandise in payment, what would the seller eventually do with it? He couldn't sell it, for again the transaction would be recorded on his financial records, and the question would be raised: How did he obtain that merchandise, since there is no record of sale by an authorized merchant? Pretty soon, the narcotics peddler might have a warehouse loaded with television sets and other stolen items, and no way to dispose of them—at least not in this country, and not without being detected even if he sold them for cash in some other country.

Similarly, it will no longer be possible for a businessman to siphon cash funds into his pocket to avoid taxation on them. All his earnings, like everyone else's, will be directly and immediately recorded in a bank's computer, where they will be impossible to hide or alter.

Of course, there is always the possibility that a computer programmer working for a bank could inflate his own earnings records, and thus have more to spend than he legally earns. And there is also the possibility that a group of unscrupulous businessmen or underworld figures could gain control of a bank, and its computer. However, computer experts and government agencies already are working on programming and bank licensing methods to prevent these schemes.

How soon will the "cashless society" appear? Some bankers predict as early as 1979; others say not until the mid-1980's. Taking the middle year of these two forecasts, anyone opposed to credit cards and credit buying still has some twelve to thirteen years in which to accumulate his nickels, dimes and quarters.

VII
"I Pledge Allegiance..."

Gregory Hansen, born yesterday, has the national identification number HUB 241708347 stamped on the side of his
birth certificate. It is a number that will identify him and
what he is doing for the rest of his life.

Gregory Hansen, of course, is fictional. And so is his national identification number. But not too long ago a law
professor named Arthur W. Miller of the University of
Michigan warned a congressional committee that if a computerized citizen-information file were developed, it could
become a monstrous "Big Brother," and the national identification number assigned at birth could become a leash
around every citizen's neck.

Actually, the basis for such a file exists already—even
without a national identification number. Right now, the
names of American citizens appear 2.8 million times in state
and Federal government files; 1.5 billion times in Social
Security files; 264.5 million times in police records; 19 million times in court records; and 17.6 million times in security
records. Names of American citizens also appear 342 million times in medical history records; 279 million times in

psychiatric history records; and it is anyone's guess how many billions of times in employment, credit, insurance and military records. Place all the personal information attached to these names in one computer controlled by the government, and a reasonably full picture of an individual's life and habits would be readily available.

It is unlikely, however, that such a file will ever be established. If it is, the data will be closely guarded and applied only for purposes of economic planning; so say government officials currently, at least. More likely, the government will use the computer in the future to speed and improve the procedures of lawmaking, limiting access to information about a citizen to records maintained by the Internal Revenue Service, the Social Security Administration, the FBI and other agencies.

Presently, neither the United States House of Representatives nor the United States Senate is using the computer as a direct aid to legislative proceedings, although the possibility has often been considered. However, the legislatures of Florida, Massachusetts, Pennsylvania and a few other states have installed computer systems for this purpose, and it is from this begining that a nationwide legislative computer network might be developed.

A director of one of these state legislature computer systems describes its purpose in this way: "Today's high speed computers and their associated communications capabilities make it possible to modernize the time-consuming manual information recording and retrieval techniques employed by government ever since the nation was founded. As a result, the timeliness and effectiveness of legislative enactments is greatly improved."

With the computer, almost all the information comprising a legislator's repertoire of working material—state constitutions, statutes, rules and regulations, legislator profiles, law digests, indexes, case histories, statistics and legal text —can be stored in one computer system, rather than spread throughout countless volumes of printed documents.

New legislative information, such as the text of a bill and the voting action on it, for instance, can be recorded immediately by entering the data by terminal to the computer, rather than waiting days or weeks until it is printed.

A legislator's access to information can be as close at hand as the nearest terminal connected to the computer, rather than hours, days or weeks away, depending on how long it takes for the legislature's librarian to isolate the document containing the particular information required. Regular use of these terminals may also help legislators keep

Several state governments have turned to computers for legislative assistance. Soon Federal legislators also will use computers, and votes for national, state and local officials may be cast directly from homes through telephones connected to election-center computers.

track of the hundreds of bills constantly being considered for passage.

Messages informing congressmen of meeting dates, times and places can be entered by terminal to the computer, which then flashes the information in seconds on TV units in their offices. Without the computer, such messages must be hand-delivered or telephoned by a secretary.

Printing of laws, the Congressional Record and other material can be accomplished within hours by feeding the text, stored in the computer, to an electronic typesetter called a photocomposer, which can generate type at speeds up to 6,000 characters a second. With more commonly used linecasting equipment, where characters are mechanically pressed in lead, only about 300 characters a minute can be set. As a result, much of the information becomes obsolete in the time it takes to prepare a document for printing.

Considering its many advantages, one can only wonder why the Federal government rejects the utilization of a legislative computer system. "One reason," says a Washington, D.C., computer salesman, "is the conservative nature of our national leaders; someone else must be the innovator."

Eventually, though, the Federal government will have to install a legislative computer system, for it will be impossible to overlook the value of state-installed systems or the use of such techniques by other countries, such as Canada. There is also the possibility that individual states might develop a nationwide computer-to-computer information network, and the Federal government will surely want to be included in that. Such a network would enable a legislator in one state to obtain, in minutes, the wording of bills passed in other states and stored in their computers. To obtain this information now, the legislator must write for it, then wait as long as a month before receiving it. Thus, its use as research material is severely limited.

Previously it was stated that legislator profiles can be stored in a legislative computer system. These profiles are brief biographies of congressmen and senators and are used to inform colleagues of the bills each has introduced, of the committees on which each has served and is now serving, of the congressional district or state each represents, of the number of years each has served in Congress, of each person's office location, phone number and other information. If these records were expanded to include such other data as the amount and source of a congressman's outside income, his voting record and his attendance at committee and House or Senate meetings, the number and text of bills he has introduced, and how many were passed, his election expenditures and expense payments, and his educational and vocational experience, elections could be conducted in a manner far different from those we have today.

Let's assume that this expanded profile information was made available on a continuing basis to election-district computers throughout the nation, and that these computers could be queried by terminals in every home. Let's further assume that a congressman or senator is running for reelection against a person who has never before served in government.

Filed in these different election-district computers would be the profile of the congressman or senator seeking reelection, together with background information on each opponent. Also stored would be the "platforms"—the principles for which each candidate stands—and the previous platform of the incumbent.

By calling forth this information on his terminal, a voter could make a selection based on knowledge of the credibility and performance of a candidate. If an incumbent seeking reelection said he had been opposed to expansion of welfare in the preceding election, but had then consistently voted for welfare expansion after he was elected, the voter could determine the facts by reviewing the legislator's record, including the text of bills which he had introduced and those he voted for and against. This information, though currently available, usually is not considered by today's voter because of the difficulty in obtaining it.

A candidate with little or no prior political experience would provide the computer with a detailed statement of his policy positions, along with information describing his qualifications. The voter could then compare this data against the performance-record of the incumbent, as well as against information on the policies and qualifications of other candidates, and base his decision on whether he agrees or disagrees with what the candidate proposes.

One possible advantage of this type of election system is reducing the cost to candidates of conducting a campaign, thus opening up the opportunity to seek elective office to more persons. Also, such a system would provide citizens with concrete information on the performance of their representatives. The major difficulty, though, would be maintaining a nonpartisan file of data, for most people tend to be politically biased—including computer operators.

With the installation of election-center computers, proposed even now by some government planners, it would also be possible to eliminate the current process of voting by ballot. Using the same computers, voters could record their choices directly through their terminals on Election Day. The names of the candidates could be shown, for example, on the face of a TV tube, and voters might note their selections with an electronic pen or the push of a button. Or, candidates could be voted for by telephone, with the computer verbally presenting the names and the voter verbally responding. The advantage of this latter approach is that it would make possible positive identification of registered voters through the procedure of voice recognition. Once a person's vote was recorded in the computer, he could not vote again. These voting records would have to be closely guarded, however, to ensure the anonymity of the voter.

"Another potential benefit of voting by phone," says Dr. Karl Hammer, director of Scientific and Computer Services for Sperry Rand–Univac's Federal Systems Division, "is that it would permit the government to hold national referenda on issues facing the nation. The voice vote would permit an almost instant response . . . on something of paramount political or international importance."

Possibly, of course, the day may come when election of government representatives, and even the holding of national referenda, would no longer be required. Even now we are seeing a prelude to this situation in the development of polls. *Polling* involves the questioning of a selected sampling of 500 to 5,000 or more voters on their candidate-choices, or on their feeling about particular issues, and then determining by statistical techniques how *all* voters would vote or what the majority opinion would be on a particular policy question. So exact have these polling methods become that it is possible to determine, within a percentage point or so, a candidate's margin of victory months, days, or weeks before he is actually elected.

Whether the many potential government and government-related uses of the computer described in this chapter ever become reality depends largely on the public's response to the concepts. "Ultimately," says Dr. Hammer, "someone will have to sell the leaders and convince them that it is a good thing; then, via the appropriate leaders, the public will have to be sold." This could happen within the next 30 years.

What will happen much sooner, however, is the use of computers to "individualize" campaign speeches. During the elections of 1968, computers were used for the first time to identify voter attitudes on different subjects in different areas of the country. Using this information, campaign speeches were prepared which capitalized on the findings.

Obviously, the technique must have worked, for every candidate who had access to the data was elected!

VIII
Plug Me in, Doctor

Fear was what set Joe Brown, 46-year-old South Jersey insurance salesman, to telling his troubles to a computer.

What haunted Joe (not his real name) was the worry that he might have TB . . . or cancer.

A heavy smoker, Joe coughed a lot. And there was a slight pain in his chest after coughing. . . .

Referred by his doctor, Joe went to a health screening center which used modern, electronic equipment to perform a series of medical tests. The tests took two hours. In a hospital they would take two or three days.

First, Joe sat in front of a machine called a history-taker which flashed on a TV screen questions for him to answer.

"Are you generally in good health?"

Joe knew the answer was no. This answer was relayed to the computer when he pushed one of several buttons which could be pushed to indicate different answers to the history-taker's question.

For a little more than half an hour, Joe kept pushing buttons as the history-taker posed queries and the computer "listened" to his answers.

The computer took note of what Joe had to say about the functioning of his body, about his social background, his drinking and smoking habits, his psychological state and his symptoms.

When Joe moved from history-telling to test-taking, the computer also kept tabs on the way he stacked up when his eyes, his ears, his breathing, and his blood were tested.

Before Joe emerged from the center, he had his chest X-rayed, his skin-thickness tested; his weight, height, blood pressure and pulse recorded. He even had an electrocardiogram and tests to see whether he was a possible candidate for a stroke—or for failure of leg circulation.

During these proceedings, Joe never saw a doctor, although nurses and technicians did assist with—or give—the tests. What is more, by the time Joe left the center, the results of all but two of his tests were computer-recorded. The exceptions: his chest X-ray and his electrocardiogram. A cardiologist read the electrocardiogram, and a radiologist the X-ray. Their finding were added to the rest of Joe's computerized records; then all the information was printed on a teletype and forwarded—without diagnosis—to Joe's doctor.

This description of one use of computers in medicine was taken from a story by Kathleen A. Rowley in the October 7, 1969, issue of the Camden *Courier-Post*. It is not science fiction; the computerized health screening center, called Medicheck Inc., is operating right now in Cherry Hill, N.J. Similar centers also are operating in Brooklyn, Providence, New Orleans, and Milwaukee.

Though computers may lack the comforting bedside manner of the old-time family physician, they nonetheless are becoming an important part of the medical profession. Besides streamlining the time-consuming physical examination, they are doing such other chores as aiding in the diagnosis of disease, helping research establish in detail the workings of the nervous system and other organs, monitoring the condition of hospital patients, and assisting in the development of new drugs and treatments.

Computers also are helping to isolate social conditions which may be catalysts of mental disease. Dr. Nathan S. Kline, director of the Rockland State Mental Hospital in Orangeburg, N.Y., believes, in fact, that "the most exciting thing about computers, at the moment, seems to be their

Although computers may lack the comforting bedside manner of the old-time family physician, tomorrow's doctors and hospitals will use them to monitor a patient's physical condition, to help diagnose illnesses and prescribe medications, to compile nationwide medical statistics, and to perform health examinations from remote locations.

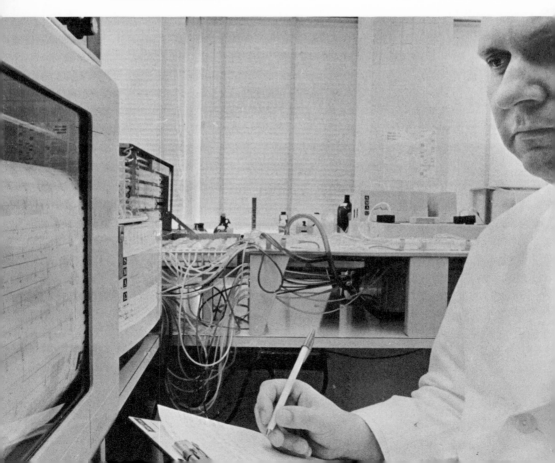

potential for 'cross-cultural studies.' " Already the hospital is accumulating within its computer psychiatric medical data from around the world. It is also accumulating the records of all the mental hospitals in the entire Northeast. "From [these data]," says Dr. Kline, "we should be able to make some very interesting studies of trends in mental illness in various cities and subcultures. We must get at what is essential in every psychosis . . . to do this we need to get outside of our own culture."

In upcoming years, computers will be used more and more in recording and analyzing data applicable to the treatment and control of disease. It is anticipated, for instance, that a person's entire medical history may soon be carried on a card like a credit card which can be automatically read by a computer each time the person is treated. This card will eliminate the time-consuming and frequently error-filled chore of recording the patient's medical history whenever he is examined by a doctor or admitted to a hospital. When the doctor has finished treating or examining the patient, information indicating the nature of the treatment or the findings of the examination would be recorded in the computer. Then the patient's history card would be automatically updated.

Some insurance companies further foresee using similar cards to inform doctors, laboratories and hospitals of the patient's type of insurance coverage. Such cards would be presented prior to treatment and the information recorded in a hospital or laboratory computer. Since most doctors are affiliated with a hospital, they could use the hospital computer, inputting the insurance data through a terminal in their own offices. When the insurance information was later matched against treatment information, also transmitted to and stored in the computer, the paper-work problem now engulfing doctors and hospitals would be eliminated; the computer would generate the statement.

Because of the high cost of computers, few hospitals so

far are using them to record medical data, although many are using them to perform various accounting functions. This cost-factor also has limited the use of the computer as an aid to the physician in diagnosis and treatment.

Using an office TV terminal connected to a hospital computer, a doctor today can type in a set of symptoms on the terminal's keyboard and have the information immediately transmitted to the computer. In seconds, the computer displays on the doctor's terminal its suggestions as to what the symptoms mean, even indicating additional tests that should be made. The computer can even describe the treatment that is required.

This procedure even now is being tested by some physicians. However, Dr. Kline still believes that ". . . in any foreseeable medical future, the individual physician will still be the person responsible for diagnosis and treatment. The computer may produce a list of probable diagnoses, as a result of itemizing symptoms, but the computer could never make the diagnosis. Similarly, in treatment, the computer will probably print out a list of possible treatments which will serve to remind the physician of one that he might for the moment forget."

Using voice recognition, a patient's symptoms could be inputted to the computer very fast. This could even be done by telephone from a patient's home, with suggestions for diagnosis and treatment provided verbally by the computer or displayed on a TV terminal attached to the telephone. Doctors also could input prescriptions to pharmacy computers, thus eliminating the need to write them by hand. Some means of identifying the doctor would be required, however, to eliminate the layman's access to drugs.

Another use of computers which is expected to increase in the future involves remote monitoring of a person's physical condition. Small electronic instruments, called transducers, are attached to different parts of the body surface, usually with adhesive tape or vacuum cups, and the data they pick up are transmitted to a computer. This procedure is used in the space program to monitor the physical condition of astronauts, and in some hospitals to monitor the condition of critically ill patients. The advantage is that the computer can continuously check the condition of several persons at once, can tell when something is wrong and what is wrong with one of these persons, and signal a doctor when treatment is necessary.

In Nebraska, monitoring a person's physical condition by computer also is bringing the expertise of the hospital directly to the accident victim. The key is in the use of helicopters to pick up the accident victim. The helicopter is equipped to transmit signals relating to the injured person's vital functions and bodily condition via transducers and radio to a central computer in Omaha. This computer reduces the raw data to meaningful form. Then it either prints its advice directly on board the air-borne helicopter so that the medical attendants on board can take appropriate action; or it prints the data for study by a monitoring physician, who radios his advice. For example, the computer may automatically direct sedation, or by flashing signal lights, the physician may advise "Start plasma." Use of these procedures is also being attempted on ambulances.

So powerful is the computer as a medical tool that the day may come—perhaps even within the next ten years—when a hospital will rely on a single computer system to record the medical histories of all its patients, to perform health examinations, and to diagnose illnesses and prescribe treatments. The same system might also analyze and record the results of laboratory tests, document doctors' orders, direct attendants and nurses in carrying out these orders, monitor the condition of patients both in and out of the hospital, and communicate with terminals in doctors' offices, operating rooms, recovery rooms, pharmacies and clinics.

Some hospital administrators believe that each hospital computer system could be linked with computer systems maintained by medical research facilities and by state and federal health and welfare agencies. This, they say, would provide the data needed to track and control illness on a nationwide basis.

The problem, though, is that so far the majority of doctors do not accept these plans. Hospital department heads do not want to relinquish control of the activities in their departments, and the thought of a machine's taking over any medical function is totally unwelcome to doctors and patients alike. Some practicing physicians also fear that a lawyer for a dissatisfied patient could subpena computer records and use these in court as evidence against him. While records can of course be subpenaed today, there is not now as much information available as a computer could supply.

As long as this thinking prevails, hospital computers will be confined to doing what they are doing now: collecting the charges that go into a patient's bill, maintaining inventory records for purchasing agents, and keeping track of medicines as they are used. Only to a limited extent will they be used in the way they are needed most—to make the treatment of the sick better, faster and more efficient.

IX

Place Your Hands in Your Lap; Keep Your Eyes off the Road

Next time you're speeding, watch out; VASCAR may be watching!

VASCAR, standing for *Visual Average Speed Computer and Recorder*, is mounted in the front seat of a patrol car. By measuring time and distance and then converting them into a reading of average speed, it can clock the miles per hour of an automobile coming toward it, of one going away from it, or even of one crossing in front of it.

Although used today only for law enforcement, VASCAR-like computers could also be installed in cars to control their speed and to keep each car a safe distance from the one in front of it. Such computers might even "drive" cars, once they had been "told" where the cars were going.

J. E. Heller, an automotive engineer, says, in fact, that the "drive-itself" car is possible today, although most people could not afford it, and just about everyone would be afraid of it. "Computer technology has reached the point," he states, "where a vehicle could be constructed which could travel at speeds up to 110 miles per hour, or faster, automatically and without human direction."

For Heller's machine to work, some form of electronic highway would be needed which the car computer could track. RCA some years ago undertook research on this type of road, but abandoned the project as too far ahead of its time.

However, twenty or thirty years from now, it is likely that people will be living with and enjoying computerized cars and electronic highways. In the meantime, drivers might at once begin using computers: in their cars to guide them in unfamiliar territory, alongside highways to tell them when to pass and when not to pass, and in cities to move them more rapidly from one point to another.

Already, Toronto, Canada, has installed a computer system for city-wide traffic control, and several cities in the United States are doing the same. The computer is connected to thousands of "sensors" buried in city streets, and picks up information from the "sensors" indicating the number of cars passing over these spots. The data are then used by the computer to generate signals which control the timing of traffic lights throughout the city. As a result, cars are grouped into "platoons" which encounter only green lights as they move down a thoroughfare. When "platoons" moving in opposite directions have passed through an intersection, the computer immediately changes the light to accommodate the "platoons" approaching the intersection from the cross-traffic directions. Sometimes, of course, a "platoon" will be stopped by a red light, for it is impossible, even for the computer, to control the flow of tens of thousands of cars passing through thousands of intersections all the time. But usually traffic flows smoothly.

In the 1969 TV program "21st Century," Walter Cronkite showed how computers might be used to guide people through an unfamiliar city and to inform them when it was safe to pass a car on a two-lane highway. The first use involved the installation of a small computer in the car which automatically "read" sensors buried in the street. Programmed with information indicating the point of origin of the trip and the point of destination, the computer tracked the sensors and indicated by an arrow projected on the windshield the direction the driver was to take as he approached each intersection. The second use involved the spacing of computers along one side of a two-lane highway. These computers noted cars and trucks passing in front of them, the directions in which they were moving, and the speeds at which they were traveling. This information was forwarded by underground cable to the next computer up or down the road, which then transmitted to the vehicles there a signal indicating when it was safe to overtake a vehicle in front. This signal was picked up by a receiver on the dashboard and shown to the driver by the projection of the word "pass" on the windshield. When it was not safe to pass, the computer issued no signal, and the driver stayed in his lane, making no attempt to pass. The purpose of these computers is to eliminate the head-on collisions and other accidents that occur when one car attempts to pass another and fails to see or misjudges the speed of oncoming traffic.

While both these uses of the computer have been implemented on a trial basis, it will be some years before they are ready to be used by the public; the cost of the computers is still too high. However, there is now being developed a low-cost dashboard instrument which projects on an eight-inch by eight-inch screen road maps for every locale in the nation. That instrument may be available to the general public within two years.

Some traffic engineers believe automated highways could be constructed within the next five years. Existing toll roads, they say, could be modified to include recessed conveyor tracks which would transport cars at speeds of eighty or ninety miles per hour. Cars would attach to the track at an entrance ramp, and then be automatically shuttled into the flow of traffic. To leave the track, the driver might pull a dashboard lever causing the car to disconnect from the track.

The car would then roll to the side of the road, if it was an emergency, or to an exit ramp. Or, the driver might signal the track to switch him to an exit track at an upcoming intersection. To use this road, the driver would pay a toll just as he does now. However, he would not use his car's engine, since the track would pull the car, and the line of traffic probably would be limited to one lane.

The advantage of this type of road vs. an electronic high-

The automatically controlled car in the foreground is following another vehicle around the nation's first full-size electronic high-way test track at RCA's David Sarnoff Research Center, Prince-ton, New Jersey. In response to signals generated in buried road circuits by the lead car, the specially equipped car starts, acceler-ates, slows and stops, keeping a safe distance behind the first vehicle—all without any action by the human driver.

way is that it would not require the expense of a car computer. But the advantage of an electronic highway is that it would be less costly to build, operate and maintain. Furthermore, with an electronic highway, the car's own engine, rather than a mechanically moving track, would propel the vehicle. If the track stopped working, thousands of motorists might be stranded or, at least, seriously delayed. If a car computer broke down, only that one car would be affected.

Since airlines and railroads—the mass transportation systems—are not influenced as much as private cars by the cost of computers, since the price is borne by many people, their use of the equipment is progressing quite rapidly. Most airlines, for instance, now use computers to reserve passenger seats, to control flights entering and leaving an airport, and to aid pilots in navigating their courses. And new applications of the computer are constantly being added.

Beginning this year, American Airlines, in conjunction with American Express, will be testing a machine connected to a reservation computer which will sell a traveler his ticket. By punching buttons on the panel of the machine, the traveler tells the machine whether or not he has a reservation. If he does, the device checks the reservation computer and issues the ticket. If the traveler has no reservation, he punches a button indicating that he wants to go to one of nine destinations. The panel on the machine then flashes the time of the next flight for which space is available. The traveler may select a one-way or round-trip ticket, paying for it by inserting in the machine a special credit card he has previously been issued by American Express.

Another new development is a computer-controlled baggage-handling system; this device may speed considerably the movement of baggage within an airline terminal. According to Ron Williams, reporter for *Electronic News,* "The system transports baggage in individual cars, 36 inches long, 32 inches wide and 26 inches high. The cars, powered by motors, travel on two aluminum rails at speeds as high as 15 miles an hour.

"Each car contains an escort memory (a small computer) that electronically ties the baggage and its destination to the car. The memory, in conjunction with central and local controls, directs [each car] to appropriate areas throughout the [baggage loading and unloading] system." Departing passengers go directly to a check-in station and place their bag or bags in one of these cars. A baggage claim stub, possibly part of the ticket, is then inserted in a terminal, and the car is immediately sent to the proper loading gate. Bags unloaded from the plane also are placed in cars, which are then routed by their computers to the proper passenger pickup locations.

With computers handling reservations, ticketing and baggage, airline terminals may soon be built which are completely automatic. Japan, in fact, already is constructing such a building, although this one will handle only freight. Based on the experience of manned and unmanned space-flight programs, where rockets and capsules are flown by ground-based and/or air-borne computers, commercial aircraft may soon also be developed which are piloted by computer.

Certain steps even now are being taken in this direction. Computers, for instance, are being currently tested which will land an aircraft in any kind of weather; the pilot does nothing. Several computer systems have been developed and are now being tested which scan the sky around an aircraft and signal the possibility of a midair collision with another plane. One such system is called CAS (for Collision Avoidance System). The Washington *Post* describes its operation in this way:

> Either on the ground or on a plane there is a master clock regulated by the vibration of atomic particles.
> These vibrations break a three-second interval into 2,000 parts. Each $\frac{1}{2,000}$ of the three seconds is called a

slot. The master clock synchronizes CAS units on each plane so the slots rotate the same on each plane.

A computer and a transmitter-receiver are on each CAS-equipped plane. When a plane takes off, the pilot selects an open slot for his transmitter. When his slot comes up in sequence every third second, his transmitter will broadcast to the other planes. It sends a beep telling the plane's altitude and allowing other planes to compute how far away the broadcasting plane is and how fast the two planes are coming together.

In the other 1,999 slots, the pilot's receiver will gather data from every other plane.

If two planes are on a collision course, the pilots will receive 30 to 40 seconds' notice to take evasive action. The CAS computer in one plane will signal the pilot, "prepare to dive," and the CAS computer in the other plane will signal the pilot, "prepare to climb." At 10,700 feet and closer, the CAS computer in one plane sounds a warning buzzer and signals the pilot, "dive." The CAS computer in the other plane also sounds a warning buzzer and signals the pilot, "climb."

Even with such computer systems as CAS, it is unlikely that a fully computerized, pilotless aircraft will be seen before the 21st century. Some computer engineers believe, however, that the day is not too far off when pilots will fly their aircraft using a combination of computers and voice command. This, they say, might be necessary as aircraft become larger and their instrumentation more complex. Rather than watch a cockpit of instruments, the pilot would have the computer do the watching and tell him when something was wrong or when a new action, such as a change in course, was required. The pilot would then tell the computer what to do, and the computer by means of voice recognition would do it. This procedure is already being considered for use on spacecraft.

In the railroad industry, use of computers to run mass

transportation equipment is probably even closer than in air transportation. In fact, the basis for such use may already be forming in the development of the "Tele-Rail Automated Information Network" ("TRAIN"). TRAIN is an undertaking of the Association of American Railroads and is designed to assist in the difficult task of locating freight cars moving throughout the United States, Mexico and Canada. Placed beside railroad tracks are optical scanning devices which can read the identification number on the side of a freight car even when the car is moving at speeds up to sixty miles per hour. This number is transmitted by wire from the scanner to the computer of the railroad which owns that section of track. Then the number is relayed from the computer by wire to the TRAIN computer in Washington. The network compares the number against a listing of all freight car numbers, and transmits the car's present location to the computer of the railroad owning the car. It is estimated that the network will increase the use of existing freight cars by more than one hundred percent.

Conceivably, this or a similar network could also be used to direct the movement of passenger trains running between different cities, driving them by computer. Unlike planes and cars, which encounter varying traffic conditions, trains usually encounter only set traffic conditions. Furthermore, trains move along rights-of-way, which are already "wired" with signal devices. Since these devices could be made to communicate directly with a train computer, construction of a self-running train, though expensive, would not be too difficult.

If and when they are developed, these computer-driven trains almost surely would be used first to transport commuters between suburbs and cities, and by subway within a city. That much could be accomplished within ten years. Then at a later date computer-driven trains might be used to transport people at high speeds between different cities.

Most people, however, would not now accept such a train, just as they would not accept a car driven by computer or a plane flown by computer. But at one time most people did not accept the automobile and the airplane, either.

Who knows how people's attitudes might change by 1980 or 1990?

X

Dinner, Beep...Beep, Is Served

In a national magazine some years ago, Pearl S. Buck wrote that the modern housewife is bored because she has nothing to do. She places the dirty laundry in an automatic washer, which in some cases is also an automatic dryer; stacks the dirty dishes in an automatic dishwasher; sweeps the floors with a vacuum cleaner; stores the food in a frost-free refrigerator; then thaws it out and cooks it in an automatic oven. What is more, she sets her hair with electrically heated curlers; irons her clothes with an electric iron (if the clothes need ironing at all); mixes her "packaged" cakes with an electric mixer; and polishes her floors with an electric waxer.

Next thing you know she'll want a computer!

Funny thing is, she could get it, too—for $10,600, from Neiman-Marcus, a high-fashion Dallas department store. (The cost of an input/output teletype terminal is extra.)

What that computer does is fashion her menus. She simply enters the appropriate numerical code for any of twenty-one major food categories, and the teletype printer immediately provides her with a full dinner menu planned around any of 85 entrees, including selections of beef, veal, lamb, pork,

Restaurants are using computers to develop menus; so why not homes? It could happen in the future.

ham, game, chicken, trout, lobster, cheese, eggs, and pasta. For low-calorie meals, or dinners for allergy-prone diners, substitutions can be obtained by entering additional codes or by reprogramming the computer.

Most housewives, of course, won't be asking their husbands to buy them one of these computers. But sometime in the future, the house without a computer may be incomplete.

Wall Street Journal columnist Scott R. Schmedel wrote in 1969:

Before too many years pass, [the computer] is supposed to become as indispensable as the refrigerator. It will regulate indoor environment; control automatic vacuum sweepers, electronic ovens, and other appliances; [and] prepare income-tax returns.

The household computer will be much more than a labor-saving device . . . It will come to dominate a good share of our leisure activities, too. School homework and other instruction in all kinds of . . . subjects will be conducted by the computer. Communications links will enable the family to consult public data-libraries, work out vacation trips, compare shopping prices, and engage in stimulating games of chess and electronic football . . . Teen-age daughters will demand extensions in their rooms.

There are three reasons, however, why such computers will not be available for many years. One, they must first become fixtures in public schools, both to make them familiar to the public on a broad scale, and to build up a library of computer-oriented courses. Two, they must be programmed with a wide variety of inexpensive but useful or entertaining material to keep them running. And three, the cost must be greatly reduced.

Most likely, homes first will be equipped with TV terminals which can communicate by telephone line with outside computers. These terminals will cost about the same as a black-and-white television set, and will not require any programming knowledge to operate.

Housewives may use these terminals for shopping. Rather than running from one department store to another looking for a coat, a dress or some other item in a particular price range, the housewife will simply "dial" the computers of the different stores. By entering a numerical code on her terminal keyboard, she will then request a description of the item she desires. This code might be a standard number among all stores, and would relate to only one category of merchandise—women's winter dresses, for example. Codes of the different merchandise carried by the stores would probably be looked up in a directory similar to a phone book.

After she has entered this code, the store computer might cause the word "size" to be printed on the terminal's TV screen. The housewife then would indicate her size by pushing a numerical key or keys on the terminal keyboard, and transmit this to the computer.

Now the computer would print on her TV screen a listing of the items of merchandise available in that size. Included in this listing would be a description of each item: its color and style, its price, and the name of the manufacturer. Possibly, the computer might even show color pictures of the items, if the terminal was capable of color reception.

Using a slightly different technique, a housewife might also do her grocery shopping via this terminal. Rather than entering a code for the type of merchandise desired, she would dial the grocery store computer and it would display for her a listing of all foods available. These foods would be shown by brand, size or weight and price under different headings: canned vegetables, fresh vegetables, frozen vegetables, canned fruits, fresh fruits, frozen fruits, pastry, meat, fish, poultry, cheese, etc. Each product also would have an identifying numerical code.

As she scanned these lists, the housewife would push keyboard buttons corresponding to the numerical code of items she desired. The number of items or weight of an item would be indicated by entering the numerical code followed by a slash and another number; 08033/6, for instance, might mean six one-pound loaves of white bread. Or, the shopper might use an electronic pen attached to the terminal and write the quantity or weight required next to the items appearing on the TV screen.

After she had completed the entry of her grocery list, the shopper would request the computer to display the names and amounts of the items she has ordered and that it total her bill. If she sees that she has forgotten something, she could recall the product-listing and select that item. The computer then would add it to the list and retabulate the bill. If she sees an item she has ordered, but now decides not to get, she could remove it from her order. Again the computer would retabulate the bill.

The advantage of grocery shopping by terminal is that the housewife might only have to pick up the groceries and pay for them; she would not have to fight crowds at a store. Using her order information, the computer might direct automated equipment in a warehouse to select and pack her groceries, or it might print out the order for a clerk in the store to use. The store also could deliver the groceries, if it wanted to provide this service.

Based on the availability and application of computers, the housewife might further use the terminal to obtain schedules of civic events; to retrieve information from a public library; to make appointments with doctors and dentists; and to participate in adult education or even university courses. If she was good at programming, she might even use the terminal to revise her budget—or plan her meals; to do this, she would use a community "service" system designed to handle only "one-shot" problems.

Husbands, too, would use the terminal for shopping, to obtain information from a library, or to compute their income tax. They might also use it to communicate with a computer at their place of employment, and so be able to continue working even when they were ill. Likewise, children might use the terminal to communicate with a school computer when they were sick, or to solve mathematical problems assigned to them as homework.

Finally, the entire family might use the terminal to select TV shows, radio programs and musical recordings. A list of hundreds of TV programs would be obtained from station computers. The TV show selected from this listing would be transmitted by cable to the family's TV. Radio programs and musical recordings would be selected from listings provided by radio station computers. The requested program or music would be piped through another or the same cable to speakers in the home.

Even games, such as chess and checkers, might be played on these terminals, using "entertainment" computers operated by department stores or other businesses. There would probably be a small charge to play these games, as well as a charge for TV shows, radio programs and music. These charges would be billed monthly.

How soon these terminals are placed in general use de-

Using TV terminals in their homes, people of the future will play all sorts of games selected from special entertainment computers. This game of pool uses a light pen to shoot the cue ball in the desired direction. Balls on the table then move just as in a regular game of pool.

pends on a number of factors, including the rate at which larger and faster computers are developed; the extent to which they are used by businesses, libraries, schools and other organizations; and perhaps most important, on whether stores and other organizations will allow the information in their computers to be "seen" by the public. "Disregarding the need for better communications lines, these factors alone place the availability of home terminals somewhere in the 1980's," says an IBM engineer. "However, introduction of the cashless society or some other procedure demanding use of home terminals could move the day closer."

Toward the end of the 20th century, of course, homes probably will have their own computers as well as terminals to communicate with outside systems. But as to Mr. Schmedel's statement that the computer "will regulate indoor environment; control automatic vacuum sweepers, electronic ovens, and other appliances," that is unlikely. Already there are inexpensive timers and thermostats to do these things. Computer control would be much like asking the Supreme Court to settle a quarrel between two four-year-olds.

XI

Rain, Rain, Go Away...

Man has always wanted to control the weather. Now, it looks as though he will soon be able to do it.

"Large-scale modification [of the Earth's climate], like trying to make the Sahara Desert moist, is at least twenty years away, but it can be done eventually," said an official of the World Meteorological Organization in 1967. "Using computers, it is possible to produce a 'mathematical model' of the Earth's atmosphere, a numerical description of all aspects of weather—moisture, temperature, the effects of mountains and oceans, etc.—around the world. This model can be used to forecast weather conditions anywhere in the world as much as two weeks in advance, and ultimately to control or change them."

To assemble the data needed, the World Meteorological Organization has, for the past several years, been developing what it calls the "World Weather Watch." This is an international weather observation network now numbering approximately 9,000 air, sea, land and satellite stations. Each station feeds atmospheric data to world weather centers in Moscow, Melbourne and Suitland in Maryland. The

Man cannot control the weather—yet. But with the help of computer "models" and an international weather "watch," he soon will be able to predict the weather as much as two weeks in ad-

computers at these centers analyze the information and issue predictions to regional weather centers in every nation.

Though usually accurate, these predictions are still subject to occasional error. But the development of better mathematical models should eliminate this problem. What is needed now is faster transmission of data between weather stations and computational centers, and larger and faster computers.

According to William D. Hartley in a May 5, 1967, article in *The Wall Street Journal*, "The ultimate Earth model would be a series of equations containing data from around the world and 'built' in levels from the Earth's surface to 100,000 feet up. Then, by changing one or two factors,

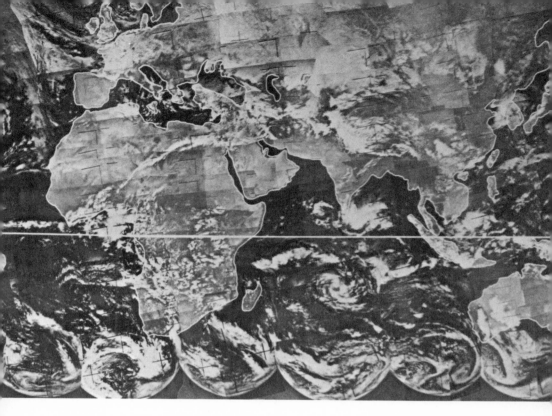

vance—and to predict the effects should he stop the rain in the Amazon jungle. (Photograph courtesy ESSA.)

scientists could create an effect in the computer similar to what would happen in actuality."

Several such models have been developed by meteorologists in the United States, Russia and Britain, but none of them, so far, has really indicated how weather can be controlled through small changes in the atmosphere. "The goal is to develop models which show what the atmosphere is sensitive to," says Basil John Mason of the British Meteorological Office. "We're looking for the weak link, the small change that produces big ones."

Weathermen know, for example, that dropping a hydrogen bomb into an active hurricane will do no good, for the energy of the storm is thousands of times greater than that of the bomb. But if a mathematical model discloses the tiny beginnings of a hurricane, a well-placed bomb might destroy it.

These models must also show possible side effects of changing the weather—that a bomb dropped into a developing hurricane, for example, does not cause serious weather conditions in a nearby location or on the other side of the planet or demolish the terrain beneath the storm. Alf Nyberg, director of the Swedish Meteorological Institute, states that it might be possible to melt Arctic ice by coating it with heat-absorbing carbon black. That would make the nearby lands more habitable, but once the process was started, it might be difficult to control it. Eventually, New York City might find itself knee-deep in water. Turning the Sahara Desert into a fertile plain might make the Amazon jungle an arid wasteland, says another scientist, or it might denude the Rocky Mountains of their snow. No one really knows what might happen.

What meteorologists are seeking, then, is the development of a mathematical model which will accurately inform them of long-range weather conditions, indicate developing problem situations, and designate consequences of man-made procedures to change the environment. Based on computer advances to date, such a model probably will be developed by 1990 or even sooner. The technological ability to make slight changes in local weather conditions has, of course, already been demonstrated: clearing airports of fog, for instance, and forcing rain from clouds through "seeding."

On another front, scientists are turning to computers to show the long-range effects of air and water pollution on the Earth's atmosphere and on our environment. Joseph Smagorinsky of the United States Environmental Science Services Administration in Washington, D.C., has developed a mathematical model, for instance, which determines what will happen as man pours increasing quantities of automotive exhaust and other pollutants into the air. One result is that average temperatures rise a degree or two because the gases limit the amount of heat which normally radiates from Earth into space. This small increase just might be enough to cause melting of polar ice and, consequently, a flooding of coastal areas.

Many states and cities are using computers to make daily air-pollution forecasts. These systems do not predict the amount of smoke, auto exhaust, or other pollutants that will foul the air, but simply forecast the weather conditions that allow the pollutants to collect near the ground instead of dissipating at higher altitudes. When the situation looks bad, the public is advised to limit its driving, and industries are told to curtail or stop the operation of incinerators and other equipment causing pollution.

Some cities which draw drinking water from rivers or lakes are using computers to analyze water purity at different intake-locations. When pollution, because of water currents, increases at a particular intake-location, the valve there is automatically closed and the valve at the location where the water is less polluted is automatically opened. The water then is pumped to a purifying station, and from there distributed throughout the city. In addition, some municipalities are using computers to forecast future effects of water pollution on river ecology, and of air pollution on human beings.

Far greater use of computers will be needed, however, if man is ever to correct the damage he has already caused— and is continuing to cause—through air and water pollution, for only through the development of mathematical models is it usually possible for man to perceive the ultimate consequences of what he is doing. Correction of air and water pollution may also be necessary if man ever hopes to control the weather, since the condition of the atmosphere and of planet waters has a direct effect on weather activity.

Some scientists say that if air and water pollution is not

controlled within the next ten years, it may never be possible to reverse the ecological damage already inflicted. Other scientists say that control of weather, as well as air, water and land pollution, may be needed in the next ten to twenty years if food production is to keep pace with the increasing needs of an exploding world population. These are dire predictions and they must be coped with now.

Aside from the obvious advantages of controlling pollution and being able to change weather at will, there are advantages, too, in just being able to predict the weather accurately.

Each year, for example, the construction industry in the United States loses an estimated 1.7 billion dollars due to weather damage to unfinished projects. Meteorologists believe that long-range advance warnings could prevent much of this loss. Worldwide construction losses from weather damage probably exceed 10 billion dollars annually, and much of this damage also could be prevented by earlier warnings.

Agriculture, too, suffers greatly from the lack of adequate warnings. Farmers in the United States lose over 1.3 billion dollars each year to weather damage, and worldwide they may lose as much as 11 billion dollars. In nations such as India and China, these losses often lead to widespread famine. A week's warning of a heavy rain or a severe wind storm could give time enough to harvest a ripening crop.

Utility companies also could benefit from earlier and more exact weather predictions. Early recognition of a coming heat wave could give them time to generate and store the power supplies needed to service the increased demands of home and office air conditioners. Early awareness of the approach of a cold wave could help them to better schedule fuel deliveries.

Once the communications network of the "World Weather Watch" is completed, now a matter of obtaining United States and foreign government funding, and once computerized mathematical models are perfected, accurate weather predicting and weather control will become an immediate reality. "But all this may do litte good," says a United States congressman, "if the people of this world, and particularly the people of this nation, for economic gain continue to pollute the air they breathe and the water they drink. Correcting this problem must be our immediate goal; then we can start thinking about controlling the weather."

XII / When Your Mind / Is Your Business

The department store buyer was through early. She had read the report that enabled her to decide what merchandise in her department should be placed on special sale; what items should be reordered, and in what quantity; what items were producing the greatest profit; and what items should be returned to the vendor because they were not selling at all.

This information and more she obtained from a computer, a machine programmed to do the "busy work" while she did the thinking, the type of machine that tomorrow's workers will be using.

By the year 2000, most of today's jobs may not exist, for it is expected that computers will be doing many of the routine, noncreative chores as well as such complicated ones as the supervision of industrial processes. A computer society survey of 250 computer experts from 22 countries predicts that by the end of the 20th century all major industries will be run by computers.

The impact of the labor force will be tremendous. Research studies show that between 50 and 60 percent of today's factory workers may have to find new positions by 1980, 90 percent by 1990. The same will also apply to many

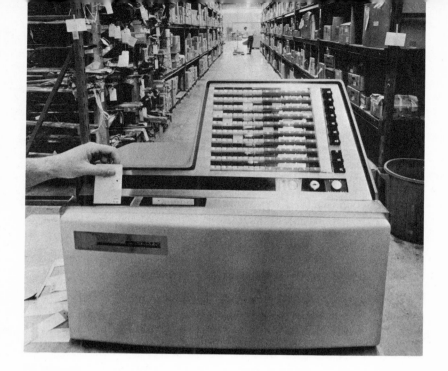

Manual labor will almost completely disappear in the factories and warehouses of the 1990's. Computers and other automated equipment will perform nearly all operations, thus freeing man for more creative endeavors.

office workers. But none of these people will necessarily be out of jobs, for new employment opportunities will open up in fields such as teaching, engineering, health services, recreational planning, government and management. Even today, the volume of technical, professional, social service and managerial jobs is expanding; one-half of current career opportunities did not exist twenty years ago. To qualify for these positions, however, many of today's workers will need additional training. Thus, they may have to take college courses at night or enroll in on-the-job educational programs.

In the year 2000, a person also will be able to change his career at least once, if not twice, in his lifetime, and to upgrade his education and his skills on a continuing basis.

Furthermore, he may work three days a week or less rather than the present five, and almost all his work will be creative.

But the most dramatic change in the nature of work may be the eventual elimination of work itself, or at least a lessening of its importance in the social order. This may mean we will have to develop a social system where everyone is assured a guaranteed income. Any earnings in excess of this amount would be up to the individual.

Although the day of the guaranteed income is well over a century away, there is no doubt that we are already moving in that direction. A good indication is our changing attitude toward computers. In a 1969 article in IBM's THINK Magazine, Dr. Suzanne Keller, a professor of sociology at Princeton University, said ". . . in identifying man with a function that can be done better by machines, we make man inferior to the machine by definition. This is the reason why computers are perceived as threatening to our identities, why machines can be seen as potentially man's superiors. However, once we shift our admiration and respect to human talents and gifts that machines cannot equal, we have put the machines in their rightful place as our servants."

The department store buyer who relies on the computer to "run" her department is using the machine as a servant. She could of course develop the information herself, and in the past has done so, but such work can be uncreative and boring. It is far more important that she apply her time and her talents to securing the assortment of new merchandise most wanted by the customer, a job the computer cannot do.

Computers are being used to free creative ability in other professions, too. Not long ago, the president of a leading New York City engineering firm stated that use of computers already is changing the employment criteria for mechanical engineers. "Structural drawings," he says, "now can be generated by computers directly from engineering specifications. Computers also can calculate design equations, as well as

Engineering structures, designs, or other visual renderings drawn on the face of a TV tube allow user to visualize a drawing in three dimensions and to have the drawing analyzed for subsequent computer preparation of engineering or production specifications. Widespread use of this technique in business and engineering can be expected between now and the end of the century.

determine the quantities and costs of materials needed to construct different structures.

"Most engineers today are educated to do these tasks themselves, and most of their working hours are spent doing them. When the work is turned over to a computer, the engineer is freed to concentrate on new approaches to structural problems, thus making his creative ability, his brain, far more important than his drawing and computation ability."

Electrical and chemical engineers, physicists and people in other scientific disciplines are encountering the same situation. Development of a new technology, computer graphics, soon will allow scientists and engineers to draw on the face of a TV tube a circuit, a molecule or an atomic struc-

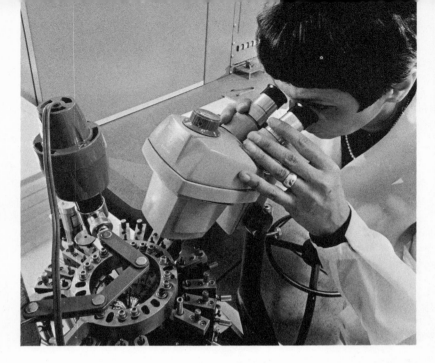

Within the next ten years, all scientists and engineers may be using computers. Most colleges and universities now provide the needed training.

ture. The computer will then analyze the drawing and, using complex mathematical equations, tell the scientist in seconds whether the concept will work. Today, these same equations take the engineer or scientist days or even weeks to solve. Computer graphics thus gives scientists time to attempt different approaches to a problem rather than spend vital creative time computing figures. Furthermore, it lets the engineer see what he is designing—and one picture in these cases often is easier to understand than a thousand mathematical statements.

In business, it is not unusual now to see corporate executives using terminals to obtain financial and operating data from their company's computer and to solve different business problems. Ten years from now this may be standard procedure for all executives, even for those in businesses which do not have their own computers; they will use computers operated by outside service organizations, and pay only for the time they use them.

During the past ten years, thousands of such service organizations have opened around the country. But most of them require that source data be mailed or hand-delivered to the computer location and that processed data be mailed or hand-delivered back to the client. Thus, use of the computer is pretty much limited to the processing of large batch jobs, such as payrolls.

Now the situation is beginning to change. With the development of time-sharing computers, service organizations are appearing which allow a businessman to use a terminal in his office to move information to and from the computer. Even if the business is in California and the computer is in New York, the speed of processing is almost as fast as if the computer were in a building two blocks down the street. Moreover, some of these time-sharing computers can process batch jobs, inputted by a terminal, at the same time that they are processing information requests, mathematical problems and other data submitted through other terminals.

Besides executives, department managers and supervisors also are beginning to use terminals to communicate with a computer. So are order clerks, file clerks, bookkeepers, salesmen and service representatives. In some cases, these jobs are eliminated, but sometimes because of their business experience the employees are kept on and retrained for other positions. Even farmers are beginning to use computers to tell them what to plant, how much to plant, what feeds to use, and when to harvest. The computer is making their jobs easier and their labor more productive.

Authors and editors also are beginning to use computers. A publishing company executive, when shown how a computer can be used for writing and editing, described his feelings in these words: "Using a computer to write and edit a book is like sitting at the controls of an airplane for the first time. At once, you are both excited and frightened: excited

During the upcoming years, office workers can expect to use computers more and more in the performance of their duties. Desktop terminals will allow them to solve mathematical problems, retrieve and update business information, and develop new solutions for economic and social problems, even though the computer is thousands of miles away.

by the tremendous power you are directing, frightened that you are going to make some disastrous mistake. Only when you get the feel of the computer do you realize how much easier, faster and more efficient your job becomes."

This demonstration involved the installation of two TV-and-typewriter terminals, one in the home of an author, the other in the office of a publishing company editor. As the author wrote copy on his typewriter, the text was simultaneously displayed on the attached TV screen and recorded in a computer. All revisions by the author, and subsequently by the editor, were recorded on the face of their individual TV screens, using either an electronic pen or the typewriter. Not one word was recorded on paper before the book was published.

These and other new uses of the computer indicate that man is moving faster and faster toward the day when he can eliminate work which he considers to be boring, alienating, undignified and unfulfilling. That this is happening is not unusual, however, for we have been moving in this direction ever since the Industrial Revolution, only at a much slower pace.

What sets the computer apart from other office and factory machines is that it can assume one job, and then take over, in order, all or almost all of the other activities associated with that job. For instance, a computer can be used to direct nearly all aspects of printing. Pages of text stored in the computer can be fed directly to a photocomposer, which will set the type and produce a filmed picture of each page to be printed. These films then can be transferred to another machine, controlled by computer, which will produce a printing plate for each page; the plates can be transferred to a press, also controlled by computer, for the printing of the pages; and pages can be transferred to another machine, again controlled by computer, for collating and binding. Thus there is a progressive elimination of jobs, until only the creative activities of writing and editing remain for man to do.

In total, then, we see that as man uses computers more and more to free himself of mundane labor, he eliminates those jobs which have long supported him. As he creates new jobs and new opportunities, he increases the need for education of a type not now available to everyone.

As man moves toward more creative endeavors, his attitude toward work also shifts from money or power to personal recognition, excellence and autonomy. Already, many of the nation's youth ". . . see no reason to work for work's sake, to be a slave to one's job, neglecting play, family and personal interests," writes Princeton University's Dr. Keller. "They see no reason to confine work to males, prematurely buried because of the burdens and anxieties of their excessive responsibilities. They question the value of work that

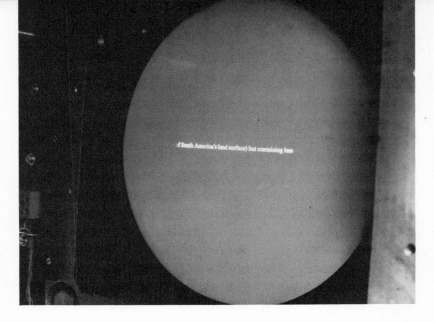

Computers can generate type in almost any size or font at speeds up to 6,000 characters a second. Text flashed by the computer on the face of a TV-like tube is recorded on photographic film, which then is processed to produce a complete printing plate. This plate may be a sentence, a paragraph or a complete page of text.

yields money, a certain measure of prestige perhaps, but no sense of autonomy and all too little fulfillment." In essence, the young see no reason to go the route of their parents.

These factors—the elimination of old jobs and the creation of new ones, the need for more and better education, and changing attitudes toward work—are placing man in a position of painful transition. Those who cling to the old concepts of work are fighting the use of computers, while those seeking a new definition of work are looking for new and better ways to use them.

This conflict is creating tensions now and will continue to do so for the next thirty, sixty, ninety years or even longer. If through better education and social programs we can overcome these tensions, we will gradually improve the job opportunities for all. Once this is accomplished, we will be on our way toward eliminating mundane work altogether, thus freeing men and women to employ their creative abilities in tasks which are totally fulfilling.

XIII

The Future Is Up to You

The computer has been described as the dominant advance of the 20th century. Economists have predicted that by the end of the century more people will be employed in computer processing and related industries than in any other single business.

Statisticians further tell us that there are more than fourteen times as many computers in operation today as there were a decade ago. In 1968, the worldwide total of computers built in the United States numbered 57,000 systems, worth 17 billion dollars. In 1969, the total reached 70,000 systems, valued at 24 billion dollars. By 1972, it should exceed 40 billion dollars; by 1975, 55 billion dollars; and by 1980, perhaps 100 billion dollars.

These figures, however, only indicate the speed at which the use of computers is growing. They do not predict the impact of that use on mankind: how man will live, and what he will live for; whether he will develop a society in which his very existence is controlled by machines, or one in which machines are used to promote the values of human uniqueness, dignity and self-fulfillment.

The direction man takes must depend on how he plans

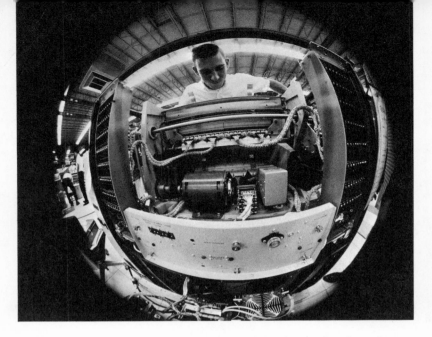

Is this the man of the future, squeezed by his technology into a position of conformity? Or will man use his technology to make life more meaningful and enjoyable for all people? These are the questions today's citizens must answer.

for the coming computer era. It is anticipated, for instance, that 75 percent of all students graduating from college in 1975 will need a working knowledge of computers just to get decent jobs. And to obtain a really good job, a graduate will need considerable experience in the use of such equipment. By 1980, 85 percent of all graduates will require such training, and by 1985, almost 100 percent.

It is further anticipated that by 1975, about 70 percent of all availabe jobs will require a college education, or, if not that, at least a minimum of two years' training at a technical institute or other school of advanced learning. By 1980, close to 85 percent of all job opportunities will demand a college degree; by 1990, almost 90 percent; and by the year 2000, nearly 98 percent.

This means that in thirty years only about two percent of all available jobs can be handled without a college education. These will be jobs which involve some amount of manual labor: construction work, for example. But even these jobs will demand some training in the maintenance and operation of automated equipment.

Although this change in employment opportunity may not seem likely now, it will happen because of the increasing number of white collar jobs created by use of computers. For example, there is now a need for at least 80,000 more computer programmers. Within the next few years, industry forecasts are that an additional 250,000 programmers will be needed, and by the late 1970's or early 1980's, another half million or more.

It is also believed, although there are no official statistics, that more than 500,000 jobs and at least thirty new industries have been created in the last ten years because of the computer. Some of these jobs and industries involve the programming of computers, and others the engineering and production of peripheral computer equipment, such as terminals. Many public service jobs and industries which depend on the use of computers also have been created. These include "mate-matching" bureaus, health screening agencies, and income-tax preparation centers. If this trend continues, as it is expected to do, there could be another million jobs and another hundred new industries by 1980.

None of this, however, will help the young person who does not have the proper education, or who, because of his economic situation or poor elementary and secondary schooling, cannot obtain or qualify for advanced education. Thus, an immediate priority of this nation must be to equalize the educational programs of *all* primary and secondary schools, and to make the opportunity for advanced education available to all.

That equalization can be achieved only if action is taken by our national legislators. School taxes must be collected for the entire nation and distributed equally to all school districts. If, for example, the Federal government annually collected 40 billion dollars in school-tax revenue, and there were 80 million students in all the nation's primary and secondary schools, each school district each year would receive $500 in operating funds for each student enrolled. If enough money was available, some of it might also be used to pay for more preschool programs such as today's *Head Start* program, or to provide low-interest loans to college students needing them.

This method of central funding, which could be implemented by the individual states rather than by the Federal government, would correct the imbalance of educational programs that now results from individual school district taxation; school districts in low-income or poverty areas would have the same educational facilities and programs as school districts in high-income areas.

Most Federal and state legislators, however, so far have offered only delayed-action rhetoric as an answer to the needs of education. They have done little to correct or even to plan to correct the lag in applying technology to teaching.

If this nation is to meet the challenge of living with computers, it will have to begin teaching the use of computers in every school, beginning at the most elementary levels. But equipping schools with computers and training teachers to use them are expensive projects far beyond the fiscal capacity of most states and localities. For this reason, too, a national education funding program is needed.

We must set to work at once to develop and implement new educational plans specifically geared to a computer society. But no new plan can be worked out until the people of this nation, through their votes and political actions, demand it. Careful control must be maintained, however, to make sure that Federally financed programs do not also dictate what material can and cannot be taught.

The responsibility for better education further must rest with the teachers and administrators of school districts, colleges and universities. Petty jealousies and stopgap corrective actions must be set aside in favor of cooperation and long-range planning. Manufacturing firms and other business organizations must provide greater opportunity for on-the-job training, so that both present and future employees without advanced degrees might have a ladder to better positions.

Linked to the need for better education must be a realization that the world is changing, and an understanding of how the changes both now and in the future may affect our way of living.

Every day there are stories in magazines and newspapers discussing different problems resulting from the use of computers. What, these articles ask, will happen to us as computers continue to record more and more personal information? Here, for example, is an essay from the February 16, 1970, issue of *Time* Magazine:

> Four years ago, a Budget Bureau task force recommended that the Federal Government establish a National Data Center for the common use of its many agencies. Under this plan, the Government's 3 billion "person-records" that have been compiled by such agencies as the IRS [Internal Revenue Service] and the FBI would be consolidated and computerized.
>
> Although Congress so far has been cool to the federal data-bank idea, it has appropriated funds to help set up limited versions of it in several states; in California, for example, all of the state's records regarding social services such as welfare, medical care, rehabilitation and employment are scheduled to be computerized by 1973. The data-bank idea, moreover, has already been put into being by private business. The life insurance industry has cooperatively established a firm called the Medical Information Bureau, which operates from unlisted offices in five cities, and keeps files on 11 million people who have applied for life insurance. The files contain, among other things, information on the applicant's medical condition, travels, driving record, drinking habits, and even his extramarital affairs. The 2,200 credit-investigating firms that belong to Associated Credit Bureaus, Inc., together have (and

trade) information on 100 million people who have applied for credit in department stores and elsewhere.

Legislatures and courts have not even begun to deal with the problems that result, or could result, from the accumulation and use of this information: how it is making it increasingly difficult for a person to escape from the mistakes of his past and start anew; how a piece of information wrongly stated or omitted can in minutes ruin a person's lifetime reputation; how government prying could even lead to a generation of political conformists or political and social revolutionaries.

Ideally, there should be strict government regulation limiting what personal information can be recorded, and when and for what purpose it can be used. Moreover, every individual should at least be given the legal right to approve all data about himself before it is used and to correct any errors in it. But this will never be instituted if Americans blindly continue to accept, as they have been doing, the technological inevitability of the computer, and fail to recognize the broader implications of allowing information about themselves to be accumulated so easily.

The same precautions must also apply to the use of computers in law enforcement, government, medicine, transportation, weather control, and the formation of a "cashless society." Through legislative pressure and personal action, the use of computers can be safeguarded and controlled, hastened or slowed, and brought more into line with the current and future needs of society.

To guide this nation safely into a new social dimension, it is further imperative that those who understand the technology of computers work closely with those who understand the human, economic and political implications of their use. As automation puts more people out of work, new social programs will be needed to aid the jobless until they can be trained for and placed in other positions. As leisure time becomes more plentiful, new recreational facilities will have to be developed that are within the economic range of all people.

"Social service organizations in this country could do a tremendously better job if they would use the computer," says one member of the Federal government's Department of Health, Education and Welfare. "But because government funds are not widely available for the installation and operation of such equipment, and because of the limited number and cost of programming and operating personnel needed to run them, most agencies are forced to use manual documentation methods. And these often can be twice as expensive and only a fraction as effective. This situation must change if we are to adequately handle tomorrow's problems of job relocation and welfare administration."

By working with social agencies and offering time on its computers, industry could assume some of this burden. But such participation on a wide-scale basis so far has been sorely lacking. Industry has been reluctant, too, to assist in city planning activities relating to housing, recreation, education and transportation, except where the use of its computers and its manpower is supported by Federal, state, or local funds.

Obviously, government alone cannot handle all the social problems of this nation, for if it could, many of the conditions we now suffer from would not exist. But this does not mean that government is not trying. A few states, for instance, have established computerized "job banks" which are used to match unemployed people with available jobs anywhere in the state. Eventually, these state systems will become part of a nationwide system run by the Federal government, so that an individual may be matched with a job anywhere in the country.

Federal, state and municipal governments, working together and separately, are progressing as fast as they can in the development of computer techniques for city management, housing administration, medical services administration for welfare recipients, and park and recreational planning. To implement these procedures takes time and money, however, and the benefit of that planning and progress may not be realized for many years.

None of the problems we have foreseen for the next thirty years will have simple solutions. Thus, while it is important that every person understand his own relation to the computer, it is equally important that he recognize where his society is heading.

Most sociologists now agree that the information revolution is becoming a climactic, crucial battle in the technological development that is welding our planet into one world. They also agree that technology has shifted its emphasis from muscle and things to thoughts and ideas.

These thoughts and ideas must be your thoughts and your ideas. With the educational and political means at your disposal, you must seek to shape the direction of your world; no longer can the decisions and the goals be left to others.

You must be aware, and you must remain aware, of developments and trends, for even though the new computer era may seem far in the distance, it is beginning right now. Under the surface of our times lie the problems and the hopes of a nation and a world in transition, asking of every person a greater effort, a clearer head, and a stronger commitment than ever before.

Index

[*Page numbers in italic type refer to illustrations.*]